◆

John A. Thompson

WITH

Catharine A. Henningsen

S I M O N & S C H U S T E R

New York London Toronto Sydney Tokyo Singapore

THE
PORTABLE
EXECUTIVE

◆

*Building Your Own
Job Security
from
Corporate Dependency
to Self-Direction*

SIMON & SCHUSTER
Rockefeller Center
1230 Avenue of the Americas
New York, New York 10020

SIMON & SCHUSTER and colophon are
registered trademarks of Simon & Schuster Inc.

Designed by Karolina Harris
Manufactured in the United States of America

1   3   5   7   9   10   8   6   4   2

Library of Congress Cataloging-in-Publication Data
Thompson, John A., date
The portable executive: building your own job security—from corporate
dependency to self-direction/John A. Thompson with
Catharine A. Henningsen.
p.   cm.
Includes index.
1. Executives—Counseling of—United States. 2. Job security—United
States. 3. Career changes—United States. I. Henningsen, Catharine A.
II. Title.
HD38.25.U6T48   1995
658.4'09—dc20   94-33046   CIP
ISBN: 0-671-86904-3

For my father, Donald L. Thompson,
the first Portable Executive I ever knew.
And for Lindsey, Brittany, and Jackson Henningsen,
whose world this is.

CONTENTS

◆

PREFACE

◆

On March 19, 1993, my wife and I were at a dinner party with four other couples. We were all about the same age, but three of us men had recently left large organizations, while the other two men were still employed by major companies. One of them, a career veteran at IBM, began, very tentatively, to ask about what early retirement was like. It soon became clear that he had been offered an early-retirement package, and that he was considering accepting it. It was at that point that Dick Silven, who had been "independent" the longest, turned and said, "You'll never really know who you are until you leave IBM and go it alone."

Late in 1985, when I was still chairman of KMG Main Hurdman, I realized that the pattern of my life and career were about to change—and change radically—from the life plan I had originally laid out for myself. I was sitting in my office reviewing a list of fifty names—partners who were candidates for "counseling out" of the firm. "Counseling out" was our code phrase for "restructuring." As I considered these individuals, it occurred to me that I was about to break the covenant that we, as a firm, had made with these partners. In essence, we had promised them, "If you commit yourself to this firm and work hard, we will provide you with a secure work environment and, in effect, lifetime employment."

I began to understand that I had fashioned my own expectations to support this covenant, and that now that the covenant had dissolved, my goals were no longer valid. My goals, though specific, had been really quite simple: (a) I would become a certified public accountant, (b) I would become a partner in a national accounting firm, and (c) I would make more than $10,000 per year (in 1950 dollars). I thought that if I met these goals, the firm I joined would guarantee me both a good career and a safe and secure life.

I came to realize that my partners and I were not the only ones being affected by downsizing and restructuring. A deep, structural change in the relationship between organizations and their employees was taking place. We at KMG Main Hurdman may have rationalized "counseling out" the partners for economic reasons, but the real reason for these cuts was that we no longer needed the same number of people that we had needed just five years before.

This economic reality eventually led KMG Main Hurdman to merge with KPMG Peat Marwick and, true to form, they did not need two chairmen. I, too, took early retirement.

January 1, 1988, was the first day since I graduated from college that I did not have a job. The feelings of emptiness, loneliness, worthlessness, and, above all, "fear" sent me into a tailspin for the next few months. And I was angry. After all, I had done everything that was expected of me, and I had done it well. But I was fifty-three years old, and jobless.

With two children still in college, I immediately began preparing my résumé and talking to headhunters. But I soon realized I was not going to be successful because I really didn't know what I wanted to do. The pressure I put on myself to find a job was, in some part, economic, but it was also related to my self-esteem. I felt that I was no good unless I was working.

What was difficult to accept was the fact that it was shorter to the end of my career than it was to the beginning, but it was that awareness that made me realize I had better choose something I really enjoyed, rather than settle for something that only offered economic return or status.

I then entered my "searching" period, a time that combined

both the scariness and the excitement of discovery. I had never realized how afraid I was to break the mold and stray from that plan I had set for myself in my younger years. And I would never have believed that I would leave the analytical, nonentrepreneurial, nonpersonal world of public accounting to start my own company in the intuitive, interpersonal work of placing interim managers.

For the first time since my early teens, I took time during my searching period to really appreciate who I am, what I am, and what I would like to become. It was a deep experience, involving more than just analyzing my capabilities and my attributes. It was a process that helped me to understand that my value was not dependent on KMG Main Hurdman or any other organization I would work for. My value, I discovered, resided wholly within myself. I came to understand Dick Silven's point: that while I would certainly interact with institutions again, I would never again be dependent on one for my self-worth. I would come to view the institution simply as a vehicle for realizing my goals and achieving personal fulfillment in my work, rather than allowing an organization to set my goals and define who I was. As soon as I began to see things this way, my life began to come together again.

From a business point of view, I recognized that I had three interests and strengths: (1) Having run one of the major accounting firms, I knew how to run a service company; (2) I had an entrepreneurial bent and greatly enjoyed the thrill that accompanied it; and (3) I liked working with people and seeing them develop. With these three basic understandings, I moved forward and eventually formed IMCOR, Inc., a company that places executives in short-term assignments within corporations. From my own personal experience, I learned that:

- Businesses were not going to need as many full-time managers as they once had. This freed up a large community of experienced and talented executives who were not permanently employed.

- Not everything could be done with technology—the human factor was still a necessary part of every business.
- Tasks could be done more economically with nonpermanent managers.
- Because of the major restructurings of corporations, managers like me had adopted a much more independent attitude.

A new breed of "portable" manager was being born, a breed that would meet the changing needs of business. It would fulfill the need for flexibility in the managerial ranks, and it would supply the expertise and wisdom to solve the complex problems of today's global economy.

Over the past five years, I have worked with numerous portable executives and gained a sense of the characteristics of a portable executive. I have seen how hard it sometimes is to make these transitions, both in myself and in others. But I have also seen many executives benefit from their newfound professional independence and develop more positive attitudes, higher levels of energy, and greater personal satisfaction.

This book is written to guide downsized executives through the trauma and pain that accompany the reality that institutions can no longer guarantee lifetime security—and to help those executives then move forward with practical planning. It is also written for those still employed so that they may develop an attitude of self-direction that will enable them not only to survive, but to thrive in our rapidly changing, global marketplace.

John A. Thompson

INTRODUCTION

◆

It happens with little or no warning. An executive vice president of a *Fortune* 100 corporation is taken aside and presented with a strong pitch to take "early retirement." Managers arrive at work only to find themselves locked out of their computers because their positions have "disappeared." Or the company you work for has just announced a corporatewide layoff of 10,000 people and your name appears on the list of those to be "downsized out." No matter how it happens, very little prepares an individual for the actual moment when he or she is "no-fault-terminated."

All throughout the 1950s, '60s, and '70s, the formula for career success in corporate America was a clearly defined and relatively straightforward proposition: Graduate from college and go to work for a major corporation with meganame recognition. If you worked hard, made the interests of the company your own, and were loyal, the organization would reward you with a comfortable work environment and an unspoken guarantee of lifetime employment. Not so, however, in the 1990s, where layoffs at the nation's top companies now average a total of 2,600 per day, and a feature article in *Fortune* magazine asks: "Where are the displaced employees to find work?"

Suddenly, we find ourselves in the midst of a quantum shift in the relationship between employers and employees. As one CEO recently described this sense of disorientation, "It's like playing baseball for eight innings, when suddenly someone comes along and announces, 'Now it's football, with two minutes to play.'"

An entire generation of executives and managers who started their careers in the fifties and sixties while "lifetime employment" was a given have been caught in this transition. They have come to understand that far from being one-time corrections to boost profit margins, large-scale layoffs and restructurings are becoming a permanent feature of the workplace. Many who have found themselves jobless are struggling to shift their attitudes and approach to work in order to remain viable in a very different marketplace.

In his first economic address, President Clinton pointed out the fact that the American worker today, in sharp contrast to the old concept of lifetime employment, can expect to have eight different jobs in the course of his or her career—a statistic that Labor Secretary Robert Reich confirms. One woman in the press gallery that day exclaimed, "Good God, I'm seven short!," reflecting that for most Americans this is stunning and confusing news.

President Clinton's statement is grounded in the fact that over the last thirty years the U.S. economy has experienced a basic shift in the forces that drive it. We have undergone a radical change in the nature of work: moving from a system of mechanical forces largely supported by physical labor to one in which technological advances—chiefly in the form of computerization— have made us increasingly dependent on the knowledge of the workforce. This deep and permanent shift in the means of production has had a profound effect on management structure. Fewer executives, with different kinds of skills, are required to do the same tasks. The abiding changes effected by technological advances on the very nature of how each of us works create a mandate for professionals and managers to rely more on their skills and capabilities to earn a living, rather than on their relationship with the organization.

Since fewer permanent managers are needed today—thus enabling companies to "rightsize" the number of employees—they are simultaneously turning to outside sources to perform operations and tasks on an "as needed" basis. Thus, many no-fault–terminated executives are finding that while they may not be valuable as permanent, salaried employees, their skills and experience are in demand on an assignment basis. This new, self-directed career path has caught many executives unprepared to manage themselves and has created a state of confusion in which they lose confidence in their ability to maintain stable career paths.

While corporations are busily adapting themselves to the knowledge-based economy by "flattening out," empowering managers, and generally shifting their relationships with employees from boss-worker to peer-peer, managers and executives are examining what they need to do to function successfully in the new environment. In our highly competitive global economy, we all must be able to adapt at a moment's notice to the changing needs of business—whether that means moving from one work team to another within a company, or moving from company to company as an "interim manager." Executives today no longer climb "corporate ladders"; they must be flexible enough to leap from one corporation to the next on the strength of their individual "portable" skills alone.

The practical effect of restructuring the U.S. economy is that there are more highly qualified managers and executives than there are permanent positions available. However, since when most corporations were downsized, little attention was paid to whether enough executives were being retained to get all the work done, there is a rising demand for specific managerial skills on an as-needed basis among the very corporations that cut back. This quantum shift in employer-employee relationships heralds a greater degree of mobility among executives who will move from one assignment to the next and a marked decrease in the expectation for lifetime employment with one company.

A new breed of executive is emerging in response to the demand for flexibility within this rapidly shifting marketplace. Best described as "portable executives," they possess both the ability and the willingness to apply their core competencies on an as-needed basis. These executives operate in a contract relationship with the organizations they work for and are prepared to move in, get the job done, and move on. An assignment may last two days or ten years—the duration is not important. What is important is that today's executives and corporations are forging a new agreement in which the performance of specific tasks takes precedence over a long-term blanket commitment to any one organization.

While this change in the relationship between employer and employee is not easy for organizations, it is even harder for the individual executive. With a decade's worth of restructuring behind us, the first generation of downsized American executives is making its way through these changes. These executives are giving voice to—and beginning to answer—the questions concerning all of us as the shape and the nature of work are being permanently reconfigured: How can executives maintain continuity in their careers as they move from assignment to assignment? What is the nature of the new relationship between employers and the executives they employ? How can managers continually make a valuable contribution in today's high-performance, global economy where the need for flexibility increasingly demands that individuals be prepared to enter into work relationships on an as-needed basis and willingly terminate those relationships when an assignment ends? Without an organization behind them to give shape and direction to their careers, how can executives map their own course and steadily increase their value in the marketplace?

Without the power of a long-term employer to back them up, how can executives provide for the needs once seen to by their organizations? And what is the definition—if there is one—of corporate loyalty today?

An entirely new set of attitudes toward employment relationships and toward work itself must be adopted by all who expect to map successful career paths for themselves for the 1990s and beyond. Today, executives must be able to identify, develop, and continuously market themselves based on their core skills, whether they are currently in mid-career and employed by a large organization, recently downsized and looking for a new position, or simply looking to make a change in their careers in light of the new opportunities that our current marketplace is creating.

INTRODUCTION

For the executive who has been no-fault-terminated, making these transformations can be brutally tough. He must break the old habit of depending on an organization to direct his career and assume the responsibility of being self-directed in the marketplace. In these pages, we will examine the pitfalls many executives have faced on the way to becoming self-directed, and we will explore how they successfully emerged into the satisfying world of portability.

Chapter One

A NEW PIECE
OF AMERICANA

◆

"I never took a job I didn't plan to retire from," says fifty-one-year-old former pharmaceutical executive Mike Fleming, but in June 1989, as he walked through his front door at 10:30 A.M., his wife Linda took one look at his face and said, "You've been fired." "I wasn't concerned," Fleming says, thinking back to that morning. "I had a résumé that showed that everything I'd touched had worked. I thought, "Okay, you lose a deal, you gain a deal, and then you go out and do something about it." What Mike was about to learn, however, was that he would be attacking his job search in an entirely different job market than the one he was used to.

Mike Fleming's initial response to being terminated is being echoed by scores of executives across the country who have fallen victim to the massive restructuring and downsizing of the nation's corporations in recent years. Losing his job may well have come as a shock to Mike, but in view of his stellar track record, he had just reason to believe that he would soon find a new, perhaps even better, position elsewhere, and continue forward on his career path. What today's downsized executive is quickly discovering, however, is that in the 1990s, traditional job-search strategies that would have worked as recently as the early eighties are no longer effective, because unlike those who lost jobs just a decade ago, today's downsized executive has an additional factor to contend with: the fact that he probably wasn't "fired for cause."

In their drive to remain competitive, organizations have wholeheartedly embraced technology at every level of their operations. Yet corporations and individuals alike have been slow to grasp the repercussions of these technological innovations on the employer-employee relationship. This ten-year process of restructuring has eliminated thousands of management jobs, and while some people still cling to the belief that these changes are cyclical, they are in fact technologically driven changes that have altered the relationship between executives and their organizations permanently. To be successful today, we must understand that it is this changed employer-employee relationship that dictates how each of us will search for future positions and map our careers in the 1990s and beyond. This applies not only to experienced executives who will be making the transition in the latter part of their careers, but also to entry-level and mid-career executives who will find themselves moving frequently from position to position throughout their professional lives.

An End to the Notion of Being Fired for Cause

Under the old rules governing the relationship between employer and employee, executives had to commit a political error or fail substantially in their job performance in order to be terminated. AT&T executive Jim Meadows aptly describes the rules most managers lived by during the heyday of lifetime employment:

> **I grew up with a "Do well or you lose your job" mentality. The threat of being fired was always there, but it never nagged at me because I knew that unless I commit-**

20

ted an act of failure or fraud or violated the code of conduct, I more or less had guaranteed employment for life.

Indeed, the notion of losing one's job "for cause" has been so deeply ingrained in our culture that, even today, many executives easily relate to the image of "the man in the gray flannel suit," conjuring up for us, as it does, a picture of the unthinkable shame and humiliation once attached to losing one's job.

Though certainly traumatic, fault-based termination is ultimately far easier for an executive to handle and accept, because an executive fired for cause can eventually determine the reasons why he failed, learn from his mistakes, and move forward. No-fault termination, however, is not the result of failure or breach of conduct, but simply the result of a structural change in the economy, leaving the downsized executive without any feedback as to how he can improve in his next position.

Though many no-fault-terminated executives have snickered at the now-clichéd exit line "It's nothing personal," it is largely true. Unfortunately, many executives affected by recent downsizings find it easier to blame themselves for being terminated than to accept the arbitrary nature of job loss that accompanies the new era of no-fault termination. In the very personal process of coming to terms with job loss, many executives still weigh the experience against the old mindset of lifetime employment, and assume that their job loss is in some way their fault. They try to convince themselves that it was due to deficiencies within themselves. As Mike Fleming told us,

The first thing you experience is denial. And then you get mad at yourself. You begin to question your own value. You sit down and identify a bunch of self-critical signs you didn't see before. It's like pouring ashes over your own head.

21

Too few recognize what Fleming eventually came to understand—that they are encountering an entirely new phenomenon in the history of the American workplace.

While it is still important to continuously evaluate one's own performance, many executives are losing valuable time attempting to assess blame for their terminations, in the hope, perhaps, that they can pinpoint the reason they were fired and resolve not to let it happen again before joining yet another organization. Mike Fleming's story, and those of many other downsized executives, illustrates how important it is to cast self-blame aside and accept the reality that, in today's corporate climate, you can do everything right and still lose your job.

Disappearing Positions

Within months of embarking on his job search, Mike Fleming's tried-and-true approach to job hunting began to fail. He found it extremely difficult to get interviews, or even to get people to talk to him. And when he did get an interview, he was faced with the frustration that there was invariably no callback. As part of his plan, Mike decided to take advantage of the outplacement counseling that was offered by his former employer. It was then that he was faced with the fact that, today, the prospect of being hired at the same level is substantially lower than it used to be. "My first realization, " says Fleming, "was that most of the other people out there with me were all pretty sharp."

Matthew Peach, a manager at AT&T, speaks of reaching the same frightening conclusion:

> Early on . . . I was confident that getting another job would be easy at my middle-management level. But I found out that it wouldn't be, even if I downgraded to lower management. It was a shock. There's really no one out there to help you.

Indeed, the frustration and failure that Mike Fleming and Matthew Peach encountered is being felt by record numbers of executives every day—executives who are gradually realizing that the rules that once governed employer-employee relationships have dramatically changed. What the vast majority of downsized executives are slow to recognize, however, is that their failure to find new positions is not due to a lack of qualifications, but is a result of the fact that there are no jobs left for them in the marketplace. "I think there are a lot of people going through this," says Fleming, "and it's very frightening, but now it's just an unfortunate part of Americana."

As Mike Fleming discovered in the course of his own job search, many executives come close to their breaking point when the old familiar job strategies fail and they have no choice but to come to terms with both the arbitrary nature of no-fault termination and the lack of new positions matching their experience and abilities. After many months of searching for another position, Mike headed to the local library to look up a list of venture capitalists, thinking he could get a job with a start-up company:

> **Suddenly, I looked around the room and saw all the other guys like me, and I thought, "My God, I'm not a player. I've bottomed out." I left the library and cried.**

Mike, of course, didn't recognize it at the time, but his assessment of himself that day was wrong. What he had not yet realized was that today's job market simply demands a new type of "player," one who can adjust to flexible, assignment-oriented positions.

A New Take on an Old Trauma

The advent of no-fault termination, and the warp-speed technology that is driving it, have added additional elements of trauma to what has long been recognized as one of life's most stressful events: losing one's job. Combine that with the realization that one is essentially powerless in preventing job loss due to restructuring and the fact that often one's job description has disappeared from the marketplace, and it's no wonder that many executives, like former Union Carbide business director Frank Purcell, find themselves asking, "Can I really make it in the outside world?" The no-fault nature of today's layoffs and cutbacks is also a direct betrayal of the implied covenant between employers and employees that essentially guaranteed lifetime employment. Coming to terms with the loss of that security is a crucial first step in adapting to the demands of a radically changed workplace.

On the Holmes "Schedule of Recent Experience," a psychological inventory designed to rate major life stress, losing one's job ranks right up there with major personal injury or illness, the death of a spouse or close family member, marriage, separation, divorce, or being in jail. Add no-fault termination to the fact that whole job categories are disappearing, and it is conceivable that trying to continue on a career path and make a living could be just as debilitating as having no job at all.

Reflecting on the beginnings of his own shift in thinking, Mike Fleming realized that:

> **I was always concerned with building the organization and the business. I assumed that if I did that, everything else would take care of itself. I championed my organization, thinking someone would champion me, but I was wrong. Looking back, I realize that concept was way off balance.**

These traumatic new realities are leaving executives confused about their relationships with their employers and are driving them to search for work situations that they are better able to control—situations in which they take greater responsibility for their own career paths rather than rely on employers to foster their career development. Whether an executive loses his or her job through no-fault termination, experiences the frustrations of not finding a meaningful position because far fewer positions are available, or voluntarily strikes out on his or her own, there are important attitudinal shifts that take place when an executive starts down the path to portability.

Nobody Is Going to Do For Me Except Me

During the heyday of the lifetime-employment relationship, when the middle-management class continued to expand, corporations encouraged executives to believe that their careers were identified with and dependent upon the organizations they worked for—and executives readily embraced that philosophy. Today, a more impersonal employer-employee relationship has replaced the "corporate family" mentality of the pre-1980s, leading many executives to believe that corporations have very little interest in their careers or in their welfare as human beings. In response to this feeling, an increasing number of downsized executives have adopted a new, positive attitude that is their key to independent survival: no one out there is going to take care of them except themselves.

Even Mike Fleming finally accepted the fact that he could no longer depend on any organization to provide him with a meaningful position for any significant period of time. Prior to his termination, Fleming's career moves had always been motivated by the chance for increased responsibility and personal challenge as well as for economic rewards. But when he was terminated in 1989, he began to notice that *any* job within an organization would probably be subject to this new set of rules. Looking beyond personal challenge and economic wealth, Fleming began to question the basics—Will a job last two years? Five?—and realized that there was a strong chance that he could be back on the street again fairly soon. It was at that moment that Mike Fleming said to himself, "Nobody is going to do for me except me."

What Mike's experience serves to illustrate is that when the resolution of the trauma of losing one's job involves becoming more self-directed and relinquishing the notion that anyone else will "take care of you," the resulting attitudinal shift, though initially frightening, can leave an executive better equipped to thrive in a marketplace that places a premium on workers with the independence and flexibility to move in and out of assignments at will. The critical shift here is in realizing that one's identity as a person is not, and never should be, dependent upon a relationship with an organization. In the words of Jim Schwarz, a thirty-six-year-old marketing consultant who refers to his independence as "individual sovereignty," "I don't want an organization to set my value."

Valuing Yourself More than Any Employer Ever Would

As an employee, Mike Fleming "gave credit to others and took the hits." Today, he counsels others to recognize their contributions and not simply credit the organization. Says Fleming, "Had I done that before, it might have made a difference in how I felt about myself." Today's executive, whether employed full-time or operating as an interim manager or consultant, must recognize that their core skills have value in the marketplace, and that employment relationships now are a delivery system for those skills. In coming to understand this, Mike Fleming made the most critical attitudinal shift of all: He recognized that his skills were transferrable and had value in and of themselves.

Once an executive fully accepts the idea that his or her skills are independently valuable, the next step in the transformation is to become the type of player the current marketplace demands. As publishing executive David Moore put it:

> **One of the toughest things to get through your bean is to realize that there are other ways to use your talent. You**

have to recognize the talents you have beyond what you have done in the past.

Benefits of a Broken Covenant

Though losing one's job at any time is unavoidably traumatic, losing it during the restructuring of America in the 1980s and '90s is not without its consolations. A generation ago, when the covenant of lifetime employment was operational and those who were terminated were likely terminated for cause, severance pay came nowhere near the proportions it does today; and while not every executive walks away from a termination with a comfortable financial cushion, several factors do make it easier for today's executive to make the transition to portability.

When the true economics of the paternalistic covenant of lifetime employment became apparent to organizations, attractive early retirement packages became, in effect, the payoff for breaking the covenant. The invention of "golden parachutes," or what some now refer to as "parachutes of lesser metal," has given some executives who are downsized out of an organization a degree of economic freedom that allows them time to think through their next career move.

Severance packages and, for some, the ability to accumulate more disposable income in the sixties, seventies, and eighties through stock options, bonuses, investments, and savings—additional legacies of corporate America—are often significant factors in reducing some of the economic pressure brought to bear on executives being terminated today. Thus, though faced with enormous personal and professional transitions, executives in the nineties sometimes have the economic means to examine what they really want to do and make choices based on a careful consideration of their career options. This relative economic freedom in the immediate period following termination is a tremendous boon for those embarking on the path to becoming portable executives. But even when an executive lacks such means and must find work immediately to maintain cash flow, it is not only possi-

27

ble but necessary to make the transition to portability.

The superb ongoing training offered by American corporations throughout the sixties, seventies, and eighties has also given downsized executives an edge that their counterparts just a generation ago did not possess. In preparing employees to function in an increasingly high-tech business environment, corporations equipped many executives with strong, basic capabilities that they could fall back on, and most of today's portable executives are quick to recognize that their training has actually prepared them to market themselves effectively in a variety of ways.

World Headquarters—Home

Yet another benefit to the current restructuring of the economy is that, ironically, the same technological changes that have given rise to massive downsizings also make it possible for executives to establish businesses as portable executives almost overnight. The ease with which an executive can establish a world-class headquarters in a spare room is astonishing.

In recent years, the introduction of the personal computer, as well as user-friendly software that can be customized by the owner, has boosted the productivity of home-based workers. With the advent of desktop publishing and accounting and database packages that boast short learning curves, the personal computer now enables many executives to produce their own marketing materials, keep their books, build databases, and do research that until recently could only be undertaken by large organizations. Computer networking capabilities allow the home-based executive to link up with clients' offices, other executives, and support staff needed for a specific project, as well as virtually every conceivable type of information necessary for research purposes. In 1991, 12.1 million people ran full-time businesses from their homes, 11.7 million ran part-time businesses from home, and another 6.6 million workers telecommuted to the organizations they were employed by at least one to three days a week. Thus, executives quickly realize that they can service customers or clients in an extremely professional manner without the financial resources of a large organization.

One Employee Versus Multiple Clients

Mike Fleming, who once felt that he'd "bottomed out," soon progressed into an aggressive search for the right niche in which to establish his own marketing consulting business. Once he broke free of his corporate dependency, Mike adopted some essential attitudes, the most critical of which was recognizing that the skills no longer valued on a full-time basis by his former employer were in fact in demand by companies willing to buy his services on an as-needed basis. Moreover, he would discover, those same companies were willing to pay a premium rate to acquire the benefit of his experience, expertise, and wisdom. Though it seems a contradiction, companies are willing to pay more for services acquired on a contract basis, because it makes economic sense—it involves no long-term commitments. It is a win-win relationship, as companies only pay for the services they use, and the portable executive is free to work with multiple clients.

Proactive and Portable

Understanding the broad implications of permanent reductions in the nation's workforce entails accepting the fact that those reductions necessitate a new approach to career planning and development. This critical shift is predicated on the realization that one's value—and the value of one's core skills—in the marketplace must be viewed as independent of the organization one happens to be working for at any given time.

Companies are less and less inclined to buy an executive's wisdom and talent on a full-time basis with a lifetime commitment, and though this realization is initially a source of anxiety and fear for many executives, others have begun to realize the liberating aspects of this new business environment. As an executive shifts from crediting the organization to crediting her core skills, she gains a sense of pride and continuity, which emanates from the commitment to applying her skills in a variety of challenging situations. The portable executive is freer to choose assignments that will give her the greatest professional and personal satisfaction and, at the same time, will deepen and broaden her skill set in a way that makes her more marketable with each new assignment she chooses.

Scores of executives in this country who are coming to terms with these changes in the employer-employee relationship are for the first time able to ask themselves three fundamental questions: What do I like to do? What am I good at? And, finally, How can I create a job for myself where I can do both?

If the "bad news" of the ongoing restructuring of the marketplace is the end of "lifetime employment," the good news is that that same restructuring is opening up a multitude of opportunities for executives that will allow us all to lead more balanced, self-directed, creative work lives. No longer tied to one organization for life—or, in some cases, no longer than a year—we are freer to choose employment contracts that offer the satisfaction of combining what we are good at with what we most love to do.

Regrets, Anyone?

The executives interviewed for this book who have put the idea of "lifetime employment" behind them and gone on to thrive in new employment relationships have a radically different view of corporate life today than they did when they were involved in it. Business development executive Stuart Litt remarked:

> The company had its bureaucratic side and I didn't like to be second-guessed. My philosophy is: Give me a job and I'll do it. If I need your help, I'll ask for it. If you

30

**want to make suggestions, fine, but don't second-guess
me. I think I'd grown beyond the company.**

And from a female publishing executive:

**The job no longer held the excitement and challenge it
once did. I had a pension, and profit-sharing, [but] I
wanted to be free to enjoy life in a different way than the
nose-to-grindstone approach.**

For many executives, the experience of having their careers
fully orchestrated by the organizations that employed them un-
dercut their creativity and kept them from fully utilizing their
unique talents. Perhaps Stu Litt put it best when he said: "I
found myself unable to do sensible things by my own lights. I
wanted more freedom."

Though many executives enjoyed a high level of satisfaction
within the organizations they worked for, most portable executives believe they are making far more significant contributions to
their clients than they did as employees because they've gained a
greater sense of ownership and control. No longer caught up in
the competitive aspects of climbing the corporate ladder, these
executives are freer to pursue the maximum development of
their own unique talents.

Cooperation, Not Competition

Accepting the challenge of taking full responsibility for both
one's career success and enjoyment, though daunting at first, allows executives to adopt an attitude of cooperation rather than
competition within the workplace. With the corporate ladder behind them, the necessity of "playing politics" gives way to a new

attitude of cooperation that is ultimately beneficial to all.

In doing a job, portable executives do not stand alone, but rather interact with other portable executives who possess different skill sets from their own. Without having to worry about the constant struggle to move up within an organization, they are free to fully appreciate the talents of other workers and to extend the benefits of their own talents to others without fearing that they are giving someone else the leg up they need to eventually get ahead of them. The era of the portable executive is characterized by peer-peer relationships, not simply in the employer-employee exchange, but among coworkers as well.

Once a self-described "consummate player of the game," Mike Fleming, because of his willingness to undergo both personal and professional attitudinal shifts, was able to bypass the obvious solution of immediately connecting with another large organization, where the game would begin again. Today, his only regret is that he didn't become a portable executive fifteen years earlier. When asked by one of his clients to come on board full-time, Mike Fleming responds today with a cheerful "Forget it." Given the benefits of greater personal freedom and professional challenge that await those who make the freeing (though sometimes frightening) transition to becoming portable executives, his response should come as no surprise.

Chapter Two

THE NEW REALITY

◆

Throughout every business cycle, unemployed executives have hung out their shingles and operated as consultants or contract workers to keep up their cash flow in between permanent jobs. Indeed, when times were tough in the past, those who opted for consulting after being let go could console themselves with the standard wisdom that better economic times would almost certainly bring an abundance of new jobs in large organizations. That philosophy no longer holds true, and no executive today can afford to operate as if this were just another cyclical change. As Preston (Pete) Townley, president of the Conference Board Inc., puts it, "You definitely have to get your head away from the idea of twenty-five years and a gold watch."

Culturally, both within large organizations and among individuals, we have been reluctant to face this reality head-on. Even though we are constantly confronted with the news that the middle-management class is dwindling away, and though we often give lip service to the idea that it's true, as a nation of workers we have either been unwilling or unable to process the recent structural changes that are not the by-products of another business cycle. One way or another, we keep hearkening back to the hope that contract work as a lifestyle will end when companies start hiring people back on a permanent basis. In the face of stubbornly high unemployment, even our government clings to the belief that it can create jobs. This view, however, can only result in a failure to act that will ultimately eclipse the career of any executive who does not recognize the imperative to prepare for employer-employee relationships of an entirely different order. A brief overview of how those changes have occurred should convince even the most resistant among us of the need to accept that executives today are faced with an entirely new, wholly inevitable, business situation.

The Origins of Lifetime Employment

From the earliest beginnings of our industrialized society, labor has played a critical role in shaping the way business is conducted. Not only have laborers been relied upon to produce a product, but as the famed apostle of mass production, Henry Ford, recognized, laborers constituted the primary customer base for the products they produced. With one bold stroke, Ford raised the wages of his workers to five dollars a day, thus guaranteeing that his own labor force would be a major market for the very cars they produced. What started out, however, as a means to spur consumerism soon backfired on Ford in ways he least expected. Ford's wage increases spawned a tremendous demand by the labor unions for high wages, benefits, and job security—the true ramifications of which would be masked by the ups and downs of industrial business cycles throughout the twentieth century. In principle and in practice, however, it marked the beginning of a capitalistic welfare state, which raised the expectations of all workers to include the belief that if you worked hard the organization would take care of you for the rest of your life.

By the 1950s, the post–World War II economic boom had set the stage for the covenant of lifetime employment to become a given in the workplace. The United States, whose economy had been built up and positioned to defeat the Axis powers, had emerged from the war as the major relatively unscarred industrial society. A large workforce returning from the war was more than willing to subscribe to the covenant of hard work in exchange for job security and the good life. The national workforce snapped up the products they produced at an unprecedented pace—propelling the United States to center stage as the world's premier supplier of consumer goods. At the same time, however, a new factor—technology—was added, which in and of itself had hit its stride and had begun to evolve during the war.

For two decades, Mr. Ford's formula worked beyond his wildest dreams, allowing the United States to dominate the economic world, achieve the full benefits of lifetime employment, and make money hand over fist. However, throughout this entire time, the sleeper of the century—technology—was sneaking through our back door. Though the full effects of rapidly advancing technology were far from clear at the time, technology was present and would forever alter the shape of the nature of work in every sphere of the marketplace.

A Premium on Knowledge

What technology did, in fact, was take the work out of labor and introduce knowledge as the prime driver for producing goods and services. From Henry Ford's day straight through the Second World War, technology made the physical aspects of large manufacturing systems easier to handle, but until then, the labor force still assembled and formed the product, thereby adding value to it. The technology that emerged from the Second World War, however, far outdistanced early mechanical advantages and introduced value-added aspects, such as computerized fuel-injection systems and robotics, which existed apart from the input of labor. As the manufacturing process became infinitely more complex, industry tried to manage an increasingly complex production process by adding layers of specialized managers to supervise smaller and smaller labor groups doing more complex jobs. The working theory—based on the thinking of this nation's early industrialists—was that the bosses knew more than the workers, and that the workers, therefore, must be supervised by "knowledgeable professional managers." The more complicated the job, therefore, the more bosses were needed to supervise. While this management philosophy was certainly appropriate, given the un-skilled labor force that presented itself to American corporations to be trained, it is here that the "sleeper" effect of technology can best be seen, for as technological complexity was steadily in-troduced into production, the workers, who were closer to the ac-tual production, became more knowledgeable than the bosses, and the bosses became further removed from, and out of touch with, the actual operations.

The middle-management class in this country has traditionally functioned as the knowledge base supporting the physical labor of the workers. In the late 1950s, technological forces began to shift from improving efficiency to adding value by increasing the knowledge content of goods and services. As computer power be-came more "user-friendly," the knowledge that was once "owned" and controlled by middle management was now more readily accessed by those at the lowest levels of the organiza-tion—the laborers themselves. Where our once-swelling ranks of knowledgeable managers were once needed to supervise the la-borers, today we find that knowledge resides with the worker on the production floor. Thus, we have undergone a 180-degree shift, from a time when the boss knew more than the worker, to our present era, where the worker knows more than the boss.

A prime example of this shift is found at R. R. Donnelley & Sons. Once, the operation of their color printing press required a crew of five or six people directed by a supervisor. Today, R. R. Donnelley's five-color presses are each operated by a single indi-vidual using a computer keyboard. Not only is the operator of the press responsible for production, but he or she also maintains product quality through a computer monitoring system. In this instance, as in many others, we see that technological advances have supplanted the need for a "boss."

While clearly the most profound and highly visible change ef-fected by the distribution of computer power is the equivalent knowledge base it created for management and laborers, it has, in fact, introduced a leveling of corporate America by permanently redistributing knowledge throughout all organizations. Simply stated, the need for corporations to retain multiple layers of managers who possess specialized knowledge on a full-time basis is gone.

American businesses have been slow to recognize the full impact that the distribution of knowledge has had on traditional management structures. Even though the shift of the knowledge base from boss to worker was well underway by the 1960s, it would be masked for another two decades. In the 1960s, while the war in Southeast Asia consumed our attention, Japan and Germany were busily embracing technology, resulting in strong positions in our traditional markets for hard goods such as automobiles and VCRs.

As we moved into the 1970s, roaring inflation gave American businesses the impression that they were growing in leaps and bounds, when, in fact, they were either operating flat or losing ground in the technological arena. High inflation kept dollars rising while actual growth was steady or on the decline. While we could have been developing management structures appropriate for rapidly emerging technology during that time period, we were instead caught up in trying to control inflation.

In the 1980s, we continued to be insensitive to the underlying structural change created by technology, as we focused on reaping the value of our undervalued assets through leveraged buyouts, employee stock ownership plans, and other forms of mergers and acquisitions. Given the climate, it isn't surprising that we placed little emphasis on technology as a force that would reconfigure our workplaces. It wasn't until the stagnation of the late 1980s, when the pigeons came home to roost in the form of aggressive layoffs in the middle-management ranks, that we began to recognize that the rules of the game had been changed and that, for better or worse, that change was permanent.

With bosses and workers sharing more equivalent portions of the knowledge base for the first time, multiple layers of management were redundant, triggering the major reorganizations and downsizings of corporations that left the white-collar middle managers as their major casualty. Though viewed by some commentators at the time as simply a consequence of the major LBOs, which were designed to bring efficiency to the bloated giants of American industry, we were too busy making short-term profits to properly recognize, attack, or plan for new management structures to reflect the blossoming of a knowledge-based economy. The challenge facing corporations in the 1990s is to create a culture that encourages employees to continuously enhance their skill bases while retaining their services through challenging work and not, as previously, through a blanket guarantee of lifetime employment.

The Politics of Redundancy

"A large portion of your time in a corporation is spent playing politics, plain and simple," said portable executive and current president and CEO of Borel & Company, Richard Borel, in an interview for this book:

> **And whenever you've got three people, you've got politics. But when you set up an organization and there's constant competition among various individuals to get to a higher and higher part of the pyramid, you increase conflict and reduce productivity.**

As a former CEO of a multimillion-dollar corporation put it, "Idle hands create politics," and all around us, technology is creating idle hands. As previously mentioned, however, the effect of technology on middle management was to dramatically reduce opportunity within the organization. As corporations moved more and more aggressively to eliminate the positions in the pyramid that middle managers were aiming for, they unwittingly created an atmosphere of political infighting, turf wars, inefficiency, and what can only be termed a "lifeboat" response to the threat that "you could be next." As middle-management reductions grew increasingly threatening, many executives like Stu Litt began to notice an unmistakable change within the organizations they worked for. "There once was a very strong cultural attachment to the company. People did extraordinary things on behalf of it. There was a lot of self-sacrifice on many levels. Maybe," reflects Litt today, "that was an artifact of the times." Forty-six-year-old AT&T microelectronics manager Ken Heimberg points to the lack of challenge inherent in an environment where middle managers are tripping over themselves just to find something to do. "People are working on projects, and when the project is over, many are just sitting there not working very much at all."

From an environment of relative security under the patriarchal organizational structure that once promised "lifetime employment" and dominated corporate culture in the United States and elsewhere, middle managers were plummeted almost overnight into a state of corporate confusion in which all previous protection was lost and all bets were off. Later in this book, we will examine in close detail how individual executives have wrestled with the effects of that turmoil on a personal level and have grown beyond it, but for the moment, it is important to note that the distribution of knowledge throughout every level of the organization has spawned a grudging acceptance that a new management model is required.

Unseen Traps

One of the major differences between the famed downsizing of the 1980s and other recessions is that for the first time in modern memory, capable and experienced executives found themselves out of work not because of poor performance or purely bad economic times—the nation's economy was still growing—but because their jobs had disappeared, never again to be replaced. In corporations throughout the country, executives like Stuart Litt began to witness wholesale cuts of very talented people, and with them a tremendous erosion of company loyalty. Indeed, much of the bitterness expressed by downsized executives is caused by the organizational view that the employee is an expense that the company would gladly pay to get rid of, rather than an asset whose intrinsic value lies in each individual's unique knowledge. In the words of a former purchasing executive at DuPont: "DuPont was a family company that, although patriarchal in nature, focused on the development of its employees until economic times got tough. Then they destroyed the whole sense of family." As corporations have begun recognizing that the need to downsize is structural in nature, they are becoming more concerned about their managers' feelings of not being valued or appreciated, and many are working diligently to restore more balanced relationships within their organizations.

As corporations responded to directives to "cut, cut, cut," and the concept of restructuring as an economic "good" grew, few corporations applied sound, long-term strategies to making reductions in middle management. Organizations lacking strategic vision for the long term failed to utilize the talent they did have, often because they themselves had not arrived at the fact that the reductions they were making were permanent in nature. As Ed Burrell, a portable executive who was downsized out of Union Carbide, put it, "When I left, they lost one hell of a resource." For many corporations, the reduction of the middle-management class was still viewed as an interim cost-cutting measure, not as the wake-up call it in fact was, signaling that the old systems of management were no longer appropriate for a technologically driven society. In fact, many organizations actually compounded their problems by creating new inefficiencies that offset their cost savings, as it was discovered that there were too few people left to get the job done. When these inefficiencies were recognized at IBM and other organizations, they were able to lure back some of the very same people that they'd no-fault-terminated—this time, as contract managers. But many of the early-retirement incentives and "parachutes" were simply too good to pass up and consequently attracted the most talented people, thereby compromising both the strength of the organization and the morale of the employees watching the senseless and seemingly arbitrary

pattern of executive exodus. As George Balinski, a former director of information systems for Mercedes-Benz of North America,
observed:

> One problem with the attractive packages that compa-
> nies offer long-term employees is that some people who
> never thought about leaving are taking the package be-
> cause it's a window of opportunity they don't want to
> close. And yet the company loses its big knowledge base
> of people who know the internals of the organization.

Balinski's words are echoed by Charles (Chuck) Trowbridge,
who watched Eastman Kodak downsize 7,500 people out of the
company before taking early retirement himself:

> Kodak is unique in that it has not had one restructur-
> ing—it's had *many* restructurings in the last five or six
> years. There's a real brain drain occurring throughout in-
> dustry—we are losing some of our best talent through
> downsizing, in the interest of short-term financial im-
> provement.

This advent of what we call no-fault termination among the
white-collar workforce brings into focus the single most significant impact technology has and will continue to have on the way
we manage our businesses in the next century. Organizations are
paring their inner core of executives to the bone. "Flat," "lean
and mean," and "empowerment" have become the new buzz-
words describing the need for companies to become more flexible organizations that can respond rapidly to technology and
market shifts.

This new type of organization needs a new type of executive—

one who is less concerned with job security, able to respond rapidly to change, and more focused on the challenge of the work at hand and on doing a quality job. Today, the legions of no-fault-terminated executives are going through personal and professional trials to make the transition from being dependent on an organization for their lifetime career path to being self-directed in order to effectively meet the variable needs of today's businesses. The only job security left today is in the ability of an individual to recognize and develop his or her own portable skills and be able to market them in today's knowledge-based economy.

Letting Go of the Illusion of Secure Jobs

Stuart Litt, who has successfully cycled through both the personal and professional adjustments demanded by the new employment reality, had this to say when asked if he would ever accept an offer to go back to work in a major corporation:

> If somebody came to me today and said, "Look, I'm going to give you an absolutely secure job," then I might take it. But the problem is, there aren't any. I don't think people are dumping security. Security just is not there.

One need only observe one's own company's changing policies and those of one's peers to see that corporations today are recognizing that the majority of tasks once handled by full-time staff can now be outsourced to consultants, freelancers, interim managers, and smaller companies at greatly reduced costs. Production barriers are plowed under as corporations realize that the ability to retain a flexible workforce offers them both greatly reduced cycle time and increased cost control. Legal work, accounting, copywriting, market research, sales, product design, and even project management itself can be purchased on an as-needed basis, leaving corporations to require only a skeletal core of full-time employees to supervise the increasingly limited sphere of activities that can be accomplished inside the house. In the words of George Balinski:

> **I think that the hierarchy is shrinking, and maybe that's positive . . . levels have been eliminated, there's a greater need for hands-on work and less administrative management. . . . Companies are now identifying their core business processes, and everything else that can be done better by someone else is being outsourced.**

Corporations increasingly refuse to commit to anything on a long-term basis in order to increase the speed of "retooling" on every organizational level and not, as in decades past, simply in their factories. They will lease rather than buy, or, at the very least, make sure that what they're buying is modular. The big difference today is that this new philosophy applies as much to the executives a corporation retains as it does to the equipment in use on its factory floors.

All Jobs Are Portable

Even though "flexibility" is the watchword of the 1990s in all aspects of business, it is still hard for both corporations and individuals to accept the idea that all jobs are temporary in nature. A job may last two months or two years, but what is important is that it will only last as long as there is a need to be fulfilled. The elimination of long-term job security has not only made every executive portable, but most work is now portable as well. For example, a newly formed drug company recently engaged an executive on an interim basis to negotiate licensing agreements with major pharmaceutical firms. The process took nine months, and once the agreements were signed, the job disappeared and so did the executive.

Numerous executives have come to the moment of truth that Mike Fleming reached as he sat on the steps outside the library—that any job within an organization might only last for a couple of years given that, as real-estate executive Richard Scott and many other executives like him have put it, "corporate loyalty today exists, but only as long as it's convenient for the company."

Adopting a portable-executive lifestyle today, as Stuart Litt pointed out earlier, no longer carries any more risk than trying to return to another large organization. "Many are fearful of change," says Ken Heimberg of AT&T's Resource Link, an innovative, in-house cadre of portable executives who move from business unit to business unit as the need arises, "but contract work is the wave of the future. And for those people who are interested in change and in excitement, it can afford a person the opportunity to experience a lot of different things in life."

Many, like Heimberg, who himself was initially fearful of the changes involved in becoming a contract worker, have come to the recognition that the valuable executives of today are not those sitting in what's left of our largely decimated organizational middle-management ranks, but those who recognize the ever-increasing demand for a flexible workforce and are prepared to bring their portable skills to any task within an organization, get the job done, and move on.

While it is clear today that the movement toward flexible workforces is gaining rapid momentum, there are still some elements of adjusting to it that will be with us for a while to come. Though they've long since recognized the cost benefits of portable executives, most organizations are still struggling with the issues raised by utilizing talent available on a portable basis and the need to maintain continuity and culture within the organization to achieve its goals and missions. New policies, procedures, and approaches to work will need to be clearly defined as we move into an era in which, as William Davidson, a professor of management at the University of Southern California, puts it, "we'll have extraordinarily sophisticated employer-worker relationships, so that almost everyone will be a contract worker."

A New Definition of Career

Where continuity of employment once meant remaining with one corporation for the majority of one's career—if not for life—continuity in the newly emerging employment paradigm will be dependent on portable executives' growth both in the ability to increase the value of their core skills and in the ability to effectively market them within and outside of large organizations. As executives increasingly take responsibility and credit for the core skills they bring to each new assignment, they will accordingly assess for themselves which assignments will bring them the optimal combination of job satisfaction, personal challenge, and opportunities for growth. Thus, portable executives' career paths will be guided by a self-directed and passionate drive to maximize their unique potential and establish their particular skills as the source of job continuity.

For numerous executives in this country, being downsized out of a major organization came just in time, in terms of intellectual stimulation and career satisfaction. In a recent article quoting employees who had taken IBM's Individual Transition Option—IBM's version of the golden handshake—Dallas-based sales representative Tomima Edmark remarked, "It was depressing at IBM, so it actually felt great leaving. I had always wanted to fulfill my entrepreneurial urges." Indeed, given the rewards and excitement of being appropriately challenged, a "lifetime employment commitment" begins to pale in comparison. Whether the choice to become a portable executive is forced upon an individual through no-fault termination or is the result of an individual's own restlessness to accomplish more in the world than any one alliance with an organization can support, increased job satisfaction and greater freedom to achieve one's potential are but two of the many benefits that newly portable executives are realizing. "When I left, I didn't look back for a nanosecond," says a nineteen-year veteran of IBM, Darrell Balmer. "I felt that I had never spread my wings and tried to fly."

While the hierarchical system of organizational management

with its implied lifetime employment contracts was logical and appropriate for its time, it's quite possible that the rewards of such a system were steadily losing their attraction for self-directed employees. The United States was, after all, built on the bedrock of entrepreneurial vision, and for many executives, both within and outside of the organization, the reinfusion of entrepreneurial spirit in the United States economy through a flexible, portable executive workforce couldn't come a moment too soon. For the individual executive in the 1990s who is capable of adopting a "portable" mind-set to match the spiraling market demand for his or her talents, the stage is set and waiting. One cannot, however, make the transition to being portable without willingly undergoing deep changes in both one's attitude and approach to work. For that reason, we will devote the next chapter to defining the attributes that portable executives share.

Chapter Three

PROFILE OF A

PORTABLE EXECUTIVE

◆

The ways in which business is moving to restructure itself is opening up tremendous opportunities for portable executives. The demand for flexibility in the workforce and the emergence of a contingent economy in the United States are having a dramatic impact on those still working within large organizations as well. Managers and executives of all stripes are taking on different attributes, skills, and priorities as they grow increasingly attentive to the shift in the relationship between employers and employees.

Structuring one's career around one's core skills and developing the ability to market them effectively is the essence of portability, and developing a portable executive mind-set is critical for all executives, be they employed by large organizations or operating on a contract basis.

With today's college graduate expected to average six job changes over the course of their careers—four of which will end in no-fault termination—it is imperative for them to move to adopt the attributes of portability that will ensure work continuity. Continuity of work in the 1990s and beyond will mean having a series of work assignments—often with multiple employers—

which build on an executive's core skills and offer the opportunity to expand and deepen them throughout one's career.

Attributes of a Portable Executive

Whether operating within or outside an organization, portable executives possess a number of distinctive attributes that give them a unique edge in negotiating the new employer-employee relationships. They have adopted an entirely different approach to work that distinguishes them from other executives, who see their jobs primarily as simply serving the needs of the corporation they work for.

Everything a portable executive does springs from a core attitude of self-direction. Today's portable executives recognize the limits of ceding their identity and the lifetime welfare of their careers to any one organization, and they adjust the relationship they have with any employer accordingly. They accept that they—and they alone—are responsible both for the quality of their work and the continuity of it, and that attitude is evident even among those employed by large organizations. Portable executive Stuart Litt puts it this way:

> My value is strictly a function of what I can contribute . . . that's the only thing that's going to be of value and make me valuable in the world—not how long I've been there, or how good my relationship is with my boss. It's just what my own skill set is.

Matthew Peach, a fifty-seven-year-old manager who moved to AT&T's innovative Resource Link, a division of the company that places those who have been downsized from full-time AT&T positions in interim assignments elsewhere within AT&T, echoes Litt's thinking: "I like the fact that now I'm being evaluated strictly on the basis of my contributions, rather than all the nebulous things . . . like how good a politician I was, or how perceptive I was with the boss and in the climate. I'm more self-reliant."

Content over Status

As both Stuart Litt's and Matthew Peach's statements reflect, until very recently, an executive's next assignment within an organization—the proverbial move up the corporate ladder—was in some measure dependent upon political acumen. Now that lifetime commitments and the corporate ladder are disappearing, executives are motivated to do quality work, and politics is subordinated to getting the job done.

Portable executives approach their work as assignment-oriented and are prepared to go in, get the job done, and leave. Often described as "quick studies," they bring an exceptional degree of energy and focus to an assignment, assimilate effortlessly into a team, accomplish the specified task, and move forward. Moreover, portable executives assess the value of any given assignment with a view to its potential to both deepen and broaden their existing skills in a way that will increase their ability to get the next assignment.

As both employers and employees adapt to working relationships that are geared to serve the immediate needs of the organization, it becomes obvious that the perks and other incentives once coupled with increased responsibility to lure executives up the ladder are less important. As Thomas Dooley, former CEO of the Connecticut General Life Insurance Company, stated, "I was less concerned with status and more concerned with getting the job done." The lure for today's portable executives is the work itself, and as they approach each new assignment, they must evaluate it in terms of the rewards that will accompany accomplishing it, and the extent to which the assignment will improve their marketability over the long term. "You have to decide," says one marketing executive we interviewed, "whether the space you are allowed to work in makes you feel comfortable, and whether the mission that you have to accomplish within that space is one that you can buy into and make a contribution to. That's what you have to look for in an executive position today. If you have your choice of assignments, you have to evaluate which ones will give you the best experience and increase the breadth of your knowledge and your skill set." Portable executives experience the inner contentment and satisfaction that comes from the confidence of knowing they can rely on their core skills to generate continuity in their work lives.

As that inner confidence builds, many, like former human resources coordinator Elaine Bednarski, realize that losing a job is no longer a major threat to their existence. As Bednarski put it, "I'll always be responsible for myself. If I lost my job, I'd just take my skill set and move to another company." The portable-executive mind-set, which values work over the organization, is ultimately an attribute that generates both self-reliance and greater freedom.

Corporate Loyalty

Closely related to the content and continuity of work is the relationship that develops between portable executives and the organizations they work with. One of the mainstays of the old corporate-ladder system and the promise of lifetime employment was the need to develop corporate loyalty. But when you cut through to the meaning of corporate loyalty today, you're left with the idea that an organization needs long-term committed workers to produce quality products and services. Traditionally, corporate loyalty has manifested itself through the physical presence of employees and their commitment to one employer in exchange for "permanent job security." Management consultant Sam Marks describes this exchange: "They seem to hook the concept of loyalty to physical presence." The portable executive, however, views loyalty as a commitment to objectivity, accountability, and results. "It's hard, though," says Marks, "for traditional organizations to grasp what it means to be able to hold someone accountable but to also respect his or her freedom."

While this need has not changed, the ways in which organizations will achieve it has. Since job security—one of the central elements of corporate loyalty—is no longer guaranteed, loyalty must be derived from the challenge and the satisfaction of the work. Thus, loyalty today grows out of the content of the work rather than the security of the job.

A Talent for Creating Their Own Jobs

Whether operating within an organization, or servicing one from the outside on a contract basis, portable executives display a marked ability to recognize opportunity in their work environments and create their own assignments.

Twenty years after joining Polaroid, senior manufacturing manager Mansfield Elkind decided to focus on his fascination with how people create change in their lives. At Polaroid, he recognized that whenever employees were unable to effect change in their lives, it spilled over into the organization. Sensing that his real passion lay in discovering how to create change in people, and drawn to the work-development side of the business, he proposed a self-designed job to Polaroid and they approved it. "I changed careers," says Elkind, "and made my avocation my vocation." Even though Elkind admits, "I took a lot of chances doing what I did and the way I did it," he was able to maintain the critical support of senior staff members, which was necessary for him to continue. After several years, Elkind's business attracted the attention of outsiders, and soon he was bringing in $100,000 worth of business from outside of Polaroid. He had just submitted a business plan to Polaroid to further develop the business when their takeover turn came and he was forced to decide whether to stay and watch his new venture be back-burnered or accept Polaroid's early-retirement offer. In the end, Elkind decided to leave Polaroid, but his entrepreneurial venture did not go unrewarded. Polaroid recognized that the business Elkind created was his and told him to take it with him, with no strings attached, along with his early-retirement benefits, bonuses, and a nice severance package that put him in a good position to spin the company off and continue operating.

While Manny Elkind's story is perhaps unusual, the portable-executive mind-set that weighs one's core skills and the ability to market them as valuable, individually owned assets, is increasingly motivating workers to apply their entrepreneurial skills wherever they happen to be working.

When Matthew Peach learned that he'd been "put at risk" at AT&T at the age of fifty-three, he says: "I felt like I'd been sold out by my company. I was aware that you should be in charge of your own career, but I didn't pay a lot of attention to that. I only began to put it into practice when I was put 'at risk.'" Peach's first hard lesson, which he learned as he hit the marketplace in search of his next position, was that "I'd lost touch with the core business of telecommunications. I just wasn't salable." Given the opportunity to join AT&T's Resource Link on a contract basis, Peach took it and soon swung into action, quickly carving out his own niche. He set out to create a human resources guide for AT&T, mastering the computer skills necessary to create it, and steadily gained both self-confidence and self-reliance. Describing the difference between his role at AT&T before termination, and his new role as a consultant within Resource Link, Peach says:

> Before, I might feel I'd had a great year, but my boss might not have seen it that way. What's exciting now is that I have this product—this guide—I can point to. It's an accomplishment, plus I get feedback from the employees.

What Matt Peach discovered was a sense of ownership and an appreciation for the control inherent in taking the initiative to create his own job. And he expressed this attitude best when he said, "Today, I'm more interested in the type of work I'm doing rather than the security I once thought I had."

Constant Improvement

Just as Matt Peach recognized the immediate need to acquire desktop-publishing skills in order to succeed in the job he had created for himself, portable executives must bring total quality management to their job performance. They accept and take responsibility for constantly upgrading, improving upon, and adding new skills to their résumés. "If I've learned anything," said Richard Borel, current president and CEO of Borel & Company, "It's that you cannot stop learning. If you do, you're absolutely dead, because the environment and the technology are moving ahead at warp speed."

While the majority of the men and women interviewed for this book ranked computer literacy at the top of the list of skills that every executive must master, others point to a far deeper understanding of the role of constant learning and improvement in maintaining one's competitive edge in the marketplace. Joseph Cullen, a former vice president of the Burndy Corporation, observed in the middle of building a new facility for Burndy that "people were knowledgeable about many things, but did not know much about any one thing." Cullen responded by going to the library and reading everything he could on construction. "At the next company meeting," says Cullen, "I suddenly became the 'expert.' It was textbook expertise, but it was more than anyone else offered, and I used the same technique when Burndy opened a plant in the Dominican Republic and one in Mexico." Joe Cullen's observation that "people did not know much about any one thing" brings to light a critical issue—the need to distinguish between the types of learning that prove most valuable to a portable executive.

While taking responsibility for constant learning is certainly a key attribute of today's portable executive, the demands of the marketplace make it clear that such learning falls into two distinct categories: learning that enhances one's core skills and learning that improves one's generalist skills. Clearly, in the situation just described by Joe Cullen, generalist skills were plentiful, while core skills—those that make one "an expert" in a given area—are what drive the career success of the portable executive. Thus, while most executives rightly argue that computer literacy is essential for all executives, for most of them, it is a generalist skill that can later be delegated to someone else as the portable executive devotes the bulk of his time to employing his core skills in the marketplace. While constant improvement includes the need to acquire both core and generalist skills, in later chapters we will explore the roles that each play in the growth of the individual portable executive's career.

As portable executives go through the process of establishing themselves as businesses in their own right, many seek education in the form of seminars, lectures, reading, and adult education classes to enhance their knowledge of running these businesses. Still others add portable skills that are not strictly related to their career paths—either to explore a different business or to supply backup income during a start-up, such as acquiring a real-estate license.

Informal learning also plays a critical role in the portable executive's commitment to ongoing learning, as often only other members of the same industry, or other colleagues addressing a particular challenge, can offer the information and feedback that an executive needs. The common denominator in all that portable executives do to upgrade their existing skills and develop news ones is that they accept the full responsibility for their ongoing training and development, find the necessary sources of information, and utilize them fully.

Identifying new ways to employ one's existing core skills is one of the major tasks faced by portable executives. Media consultant Dave Moore identified the core skills he'd used making package sales for a major publisher, and leapt over to the buying side of the business when he went out on his own. "When I was in publishing," says Moore, "I was in the business of selling something, but now, I'm on the other side of it. I'm on the client's side, helping him do business more effectively." Ultimately, learning to apply one's skills in a different way, as Moore did, is far easier and more cost-effective than attempting to acquire entirely new core skills.

The Flexibility to Respond Rapidly

"Adaptability to a changing environment is really the best life skill you can possess," said one high-level corporate development officer, and as the effects of technology shorten the cycle time of producing virtually every product and service on the market, the portable executive who can rapidly adapt to and address the needs of any given client is the one likeliest to surpass baseline performance levels. As newly lean corporations attempt to address market demands for shorter and shorter cycle times, there is an exponential rise in the need for portable executives who can respond rapidly to the demands of an assignment with specific expertise and willingly terminate the relationship with an employer as soon as the mission is accomplished.

As Joe Cullen moved into his first position as a portable executive—a warehouse manager on a short-term assignment—he highlighted the rewards of constantly improving his skills as he worked and being able to apply them in another environment than the Burndy Corporation:

> **I was doing things I never did before—training, calling the shots, and approving payroll. I walked away confident. I got a lot of help getting the job done, but I motivated people. I made it happen and I'm proud of it.**

Possessing the flexibility to apply one's core skills, wherever one happens to be, is a natural outgrowth of developing the other attributes of portability mentioned so far in this chapter. Indeed, portability is built on the early recognition that one's core skills are both transferrable and marketable and not dependent on any one organization. Prioritizing the work at hand over and above any other considerations in one's work environment is yet another natural outgrowth of taking responsibility for one's career, as are the equally important attributes of being dedicated to constant improvement of those skills and, above all, adopting a flexible approach to applying them in the marketplace.

Pursuing Passion

When asked what advice they would give to young executives mapping their careers today, the executives interviewed for this book almost unanimously responded with some variation of the philosophy that world-renowned mythologist Joseph Campbell termed "following your bliss." Daphne Gill, a thirty-two-year-old communications manager, says:

> **Decide what your passion is, because as long as you have passion for something, you'll come up with all the energy, motivation, and opportunities to go and make things happen. As long as I'm aware of my values and my passion and they're aligned with a need in the marketplace, I'm going to be highly successful.**

Though Gill's words may sound to some like a pipe dream—or an ideal that cannot be achieved by most—one look at the changed nature of work in the 1990s and beyond should point to the vastly increased odds of being able to do exactly that. The outsourcing of America that we are witnessing in the wake of recent downsizings has, as one of its most salient features, a tremendous demand for highly specialized executive talent, and portable executives, freed from the overarching political concerns and frustrations that were an inevitable part of the lifetime-employment commitment, are increasingly able to couple their passions with their core skills and sell them on the open market. And as portability increases the emphasis on individual performance, passion for what one is doing drives that performance. "It's very simple," says one individual management consultant. "If you don't like what you are doing, you won't drive yourself to do it."

Not all executives, however, can readily identify where their passion lies. In recent decades, the premium placed on finding one organization to stay with for life often obscured the wants and needs of the individual. In trying to identify the next step on his career path, John Pehrson, who left DuPont after twenty-one years, illustrates that the questions are the same for all executives:

> **The way I've been dealing with it is by doing a lot of personal work—in terms of my own logical and nonlogical processes. I'm getting down on paper what my skills are, what I have done best, and what things I have a passion for, to see if there's a common thread there.**

If there is an aspect of acquiring a portable-executive mind-set that is as compelling as the necessity to be independently successful in today's global economy, it is the way in which adopting these attributes brings an individual's entire life into a more balanced and even holistic mode, where passion and action become one motion.

An End to Bashfulness

As the attributes of portability bring executives' values and passion into line with what they can do best, and they begin to identify market niches where their unique talents can best be utilized, the process of marketing becomes less and less a "sales job" and more a confident statement of ability, accomplishments, and purpose. A critical shift takes place in the focus of the portable executive's marketing efforts: a shift from political marketing to substantive marketing, a direct result of the portable executive's alignment of passion and expertise.

Pushed by a number of his colleagues to employ telemarketing in his business, executive Manny Elkind initially resisted the idea out of sheer disgust:

> **I always had a vision of sales people as being slimy. Most of them would sell you half a chicken if they could, and there I was in this position of trying to be what I abhorred. But then I started to think about what I was doing . . . what my purpose in life was and what my role should be . . . and suddenly it became very clear: What I do when I talk to people, is literally make available to them some very important information and give them some opportunities to learn. It's a shift from "I want your business" to "I can help you," which is less selfish. And if you don't need what I've got, other people you know probably do.**

In chapter one, we heard Mike Fleming say, "Before, I gave credit to others and I took the hits." For the portable executive, taking credit is essential, for without effective self-marketing, his or her career would be nonexistent. Another executive explained, "If I don't kick the eagle off the limb, nothing happens." That concept applies as much to self-marketing as it does to accomplishing an assignment. Given the portable executive's alignment of personal goals, passion, and self-confidence with the needs of the marketplace, there is no longer a place for modesty.

A successful portable executive must let the world know what he's doing—through networking, affiliation with professional organizations, and targeted marketing strategies that run the gamut from giving media interviews, distributing newsletters, and giving lectures and speeches to launching direct-mail campaigns, making sales calls to corporations, and buying advertising. For many executives who spent the majority of their careers within corporations whose marketing departments customarily handled this type of work, developing the ability to market does not come easily. If, however, self-marketing springs from a solid and passionate commitment to what an executive is doing—as it clearly does for David Moore and Manny Elkind—then the skill of self-marketing becomes yet another integrated attribute of being portable.

Developing Strategic Alliances

Though large organizations once offered a sense of team spirit and camaraderie, competition within corporations often worked against interpersonal cooperation. In the absence of that competition, however, portable executives are discovering that, as Daphne Gill put it:

> **Self-directed people don't need to compete—they need to develop important, complementary peer relationships. Even hard-chargers who have been downsized discover the importance of their peer relationships and become much more willing to support other people.**

What our interviews reveal is that one of the first positive by-products of downsizing is a willingness to help other no-fault–terminated individuals. Mike Fleming reflects on his own new-found willingness to support other people: "When I was responsible for an organization and someone said 'Help me,' I did it begrudgingly. Today, I help anyone I can." What may have begun as the recognition that all downsized executives are in the same boat and in a position to help each other through networking, is rapidly evolving into a far more profound atmosphere of cooperation among portable executives. It is not only the large organizations that recognize and utilize the wisdom and experience that

59

portable executives bring to the marketplace, but also other portable executives seeking to augment their core skills through the formation of working alliances.

Alliances between and among portable executives cover a broad range of relationships, from the standard partner association to alliances formed strictly for an individual project and then disbanded as soon as the project is complete. Since being portable doesn't require the expense and complications of long-term commitment, it is possible for portable executives to assemble whatever type and size of team a given assignment demands. These alliances allow portable executives to maximize their ability and respond to shorter cycle times in a way that is just as competitive as the services a small-to-medium-sized, permanently configured company can offer—if not more so.

Beneath the growing cooperation between and among portable executives is the acknowledgment that core competencies among individual portable executives are vastly different, and, rather than resulting in a competitive atmosphere as they might within a large organization, lead instead to mutually beneficial relationships characterized by a dedication to common goals, mutuality, and respect. Ultimately, the most successful strategic alliances will be those formed between portable executives whose commitments to constant learning and the quality of service they provide are equivalent.

The Portable Executive as a Business

The same technology that gave rise to today's downsizings has also made it possible for individual portable executives to set up global, world-class organizations almost overnight, and the portable executive must be administratively self-sufficient in order to compete. It is no longer necessary to retain a multinational organization to meet market demands, since technology has brought the resources once thought to be "owned" by such organizations to an individual's fingertips, and portable executives are now in the position to buy anything they need to service clients globally.

In developing this particular attribute of self-sufficiency, it is important once again to separate core competencies from generalist skills, and wherever possible, enlist the support of other portable executives and support staff in order to maximize time spent on applying core competencies in the market.

Many newly portable executives initially attempt, with the aid of technology, to run their businesses solo. Soon, however, the economics of doing this make it clear that long-term growth is dependent on leveraging business by adding other individuals to handle those responsibilities not directly related to the individual portable executive's core competencies. Practicing what they preach by outsourcing generalist skills makes good economic sense in that it allows portable executives to spend the majority of their time pursuing assignments that directly concern and utilize their core skills.

It is essential for the portable executive to recognize the truth in the old saw "You have to give gelt to get gelt." And while this may not, at times, be cost-effective to the portable executive—as when he or she subcontracts a job to a colleague and receives little or no net return on that assignment because of the cost of outsourcing—the net benefit realized over time eventually far outweighs the net returns of attempting to operate solo. When it comes to outsourcing, quality control is every bit as important to the portable executive as it is to a major corporation, and the portable executive must choose associates with extreme care.

Compensation as a Function of Value Given and Received

The portable executive's approach to compensation varies with each individual, but one element of compensation common among all portable executives is that it is always performance-oriented. And since organizations do not provide benefits, or any form of base compensation for portable executives, the individual must factor these costs into the fee charged to the client. While later chapters will deal in detail with the economics of pricing, some preliminary pricing considerations are essential to understanding portability itself. Since the portable executive approaches "his life as his work" rather than "his work as his life," factors other than cash and benefits carry equal weight in the formula a portable executive uses to arrive at adequate compensation.

Some portable executives, like Matthew Peach, routinely expect the client to provide project-related materials, such as the software packages he uses to create human resources brochures. Others may be willing to take lesser compensation because they are unwilling to relocate. Still others may wish to strengthen certain skills and would therefore be willing to take a lower-priced assignment occasionally to increase these skills, thus investing in their ability to apply new skills in later assignments. The newly portable executive will distinguish herself from the competition more through added value than through price. In evaluating all of these factors that enter into compensation, the ultimate aim of the portable executive is to achieve a balance of value given and received.

The process of evaluating compensation in terms of value given and received is equally important for the executive working full-time within an organization, because as benefits packages and perks are reduced, or paid for in part by the employee, the elements of compensation are changing within organizations as well. The organization employee recognizes that the same factors that apply to a portable executive's formula for compensation apply to her as well.

While the issue of compensation will be handled later in the book from a strictly economic point of view, we are addressing it here as an attribute of portability, to emphasize the point that the portable executive must accept the responsibility for being self-sufficient apart from expenses that are directly assignment-related. For executives long used to the benefits and perks that were part of the job package within an organization, this can be difficult to adjust to, but, ultimately, all forms of compensation received must be a function of the assignment accomplished.

In assessing the value of a given assignment, it is important to remember that both reinforcing one's existing core skills and acquiring new skills must be considered an economic factor. An assignment that offers a portable executive the opportunity to strengthen her core competencies can only make her more marketable. On occasion, such "compensation" justifies accepting an occasional assignment for less financial reward than is usual.

The Path

While the necessity to develop the attributes of portability is clear, often the path an individual takes in developing them is difficult. But the changes necessary to become truly portable are not simply changes in one's outward professional life, but far deeper changes that involve confronting those fears about being completely independent of the protection once offered by the umbrella of lifetime employment.

The most significant shift involves reexamining the organization as a source of security and realizing that today, one's own abilities are the only real source of security. And as we have seen, the relative protection offered by large organizations pales in comparison to the quality of life most portable executives now enjoy within the new employer-employee relationships. Making the critical transition from thinking that the organization should supply what we need to understanding that we, alone, must take responsibility for our lives involves a great deal more than simply accepting, intellectually, the terms and changes involved. For this reason, the next section of this book is devoted to making it through the emotional changes of becoming portable.

Chapter Four

BREAKING THE HABIT

◆

Not long ago, John Thompson met with a partner in a large public-accounting firm who had just been asked to take early retirement at age forty-eight. Despite being a profit maker for the firm and holding a superb track record in client services, he'd fallen victim to the downsizing of the partnership. As John talked to the man about his confusion and anger, John tried to explain that the period of desperation and vulnerability would pass and asked how the man was handling the situation. The partner answered (with some pride) that "rather than sit home and worry about things, I am getting up every morning at the usual time, putting on a suit, leaving for the office, and getting to my desk by 9 A.M. I've got a plan to find a new position." Asked why he was doing this, he replied, "So I won't get out of the habit."

Customer service executive Fred Tritschler, on the other hand, took a different approach. After deciding to take IBM's Individual Retirement Option, Tritschler was leaving his office one afternoon at 3 P.M. when his boss passed him in the hallway and asked, "Where are you going?" Fred replied, "I'm breaking the habit."

Working within a large organization for most of one's career results in a host of habits. The hours an executive works are fixed by the organization, one's dress is dictated by an unwritten code, and often one's office size is determined by his or her status within the company. Executives also become accustomed to what they can or cannot say in meetings and in their correspondence, and access to information necessary to perform their jobs is limited by a hierarchical information distribution system. Many executives view their organization's policies, rules, and regulations as an intricate part of their support and security system. Faced with the sudden shock of being no-fault-terminated, it's hardly surprising that large numbers of them, like John's friend in public accounting, initially continue those same habits as they begin searching for new career opportunities. But if executives are going to change both their view and their way of working, they must learn that these "old world" habits need to be put aside to become successfully self-directed.

Though breaking these habits may be painful, confusing, and often disorienting, all executives, employed or unemployed, must make this adjustment, because while these habits defined security as it was provided by an organization, they no longer have value today as part of one's external support and security system. Separating oneself from the habits of a lifetime, however, is no easy task. It's hard enough for most people to adapt when they take retirement at a normal age. But when an executive is forced to take early retirement or is no-fault-terminated, often it happens without warning. In an article entitled "Survivor," Judi Dash, a onetime newspaper editor, described just how quickly she was downsized:

> **There was something wrong with my office computer. . . . When I typed in my secret password, neon-green letters blinked: "No such device." . . . Suddenly, it hit me: I was one of them.**

For many no-fault–terminated executives, it is usually the way in which the termination is handled that upsets them the most. When Joe Cullen chose to leave the Burndy Corporation, the human resources representative he spoke with asked, *"What are you going to do when you grow up?"* Joe describes how this made him feel:

> The statement jolted me. I felt he was saying I wasn't mature. I was nervous about leaving, but I wanted to be relieved of my contract. When I asked whether I could be relieved of it, he said, "Certainly," because where was a person with twenty-nine years' experience at the same company going to find a job in this environment? I was angry.

Even when an executive does plan his own exit, as engineering manager Stu Litt did when he decided to leave Hazeltine after twenty-four years, the initial process of separating from the organization can be extremely traumatic:

> I was an emotional wreck. I gave notice and was beside myself for a number of weeks afterward. It was like getting divorced.

Even those who have a position waiting for them cannot escape the trauma of being downsized. In the words of Union Carbide executive Frank Purcell:

> When they told me they'd give me a year and a half to get out, it was music to my ears. But when the moment came, there was a jolt. I don't know what divorce is like, but after thirty-two years of working at the same place, there is an umbilicus to the company and you really feel

it when it's cut. You're leaving a womb of sorts—a good, secure place. And all your closest friends are there. It's a very heart-wrenching experience.

How, then, does an executive break the organizational habits in the sudden absence of a clearly defined role and the measures of achievement that attend accomplishment within an organization?

Many of the executives we talked to had come to take for granted certain elements of life within large organizations: long-term job security, the ability to raise their families, pay their mortgages, and enjoy a certain social status. Therefore, most found themselves inadequately prepared to come to terms with being more self-directed, and, as their stories show, each of their transitions is characterized by individual and distinct circumstances.

Cold-Water Firing

The most devastating circumstance is, of course, the type of "cold water" firing described earlier by Judi Dash, where an executive arrives at work only to have their computer declare them *persona non grata*. Less drastic downsizing methods, however, can be equally disturbing—such as when an executive's name appears on a list of employees to be outplaced, or when one is suddenly presented with a very strong pitch to accept a package and is in no way prepared or willing to leave. The shock involved in this type of termination can launch even the most imperturbable executive into a panic, particularly if he or she has serious financial obligations such as children in college, a large mortgage, or financially dependent parents. Though panic is often irrational and unreasonable, given one's true capabilities and financial position, it is a very real feeling and many executives submit to it before they decide to assess the reality of their situation. For this reason, it is very important to recognize that while a sense of panic is common, upon close examination, it is usually illogical or even groundless.

Perhaps the hardest-hit by a cold-water firing are those who believed themselves untouchable. Former executive vice president of the Dun & Bradstreet Corporation, Richard Swank, had been with Dun & Bradstreet for twenty-five years when his position was consolidated:

> Certainly, being an executive vice president of the corporation and having been responsible for a very large chunk of business—nearly seven hundred million dollars of revenue—I thought I was secure. I guess I was wrong.

When executives who believe themselves too important to be downsized are, it often destroys the uniqueness they felt in being part of the organization in the first place. These people learn the hard lesson that if you derive your identity from an organization, you give the organization the power to take it away.

The Bouncing-Ball Syndrome

Dave Moore, a publishing executive downsized out of the Hearst Corporation, understood that his termination was part of a radically changing business environment, not the result of anything he did or didn't do. He remembers explaining this new climate to his parents when he lost his job:

> My parents had felt very proud telling their friends I was a VP at Hearst Corporation. During my dad's career, it was unthinkable to be fired from a corporation, so I really had to explain that in today's corporate culture, being fired is not a social stigma—nor is it based on performance.

Understanding the changed business climate, however, wasn't enough. When a nationwide broadcast company offered Moore a new position, he thought, "This is terrific." Very shortly after he signed on, however, Dave Moore found himself saying, "This is not so terrific," because his new company was engaged in its own resizing. "Today," says Moore, "I wouldn't be so quick to jump."

Dave Moore and those like him who fall into the bouncing-ball category lack the awareness of themselves and their own unique abilities that can only come from a conscientious, albeit difficult, commitment to truly separating oneself from the organization. Only when that process is complete can a portable executive assess whether an assignment or job truly represents the best alignment of goals and opportunities for his particular core skills.

Unfortunately, the bouncing-ball phenomenon affects many executives more than once, as they move from job to job trying to avoid the panic, confusion, and pain caused by no-fault termination. In fact, the bouncing-ball syndrome is one of the clearest indicators that cosmetic changes in behavior will not allow an individual to operate successfully as a portable executive; the process of becoming portable truly begins only when one is willing to come to grips with the fact that deep and permanent change is necessary. For these reasons, the individual who has recently been no-fault-terminated should assess whether the pressures to get another job immediately are realistic. If they aren't, he should take time to evaluate what it is he really wants to do. The "get a job at any cost" syndrome can retard all further growth toward becoming more self-directed, so it is important for the portable executive to view this time spent as an investment in his career and not as idly spent downtime.

Becoming Portable in Your Current Position

Some individuals actually recognize the need for change within themselves while they are still gainfully employed. For example, an executive may want more independence to evolve on his own, rather than depend on an employer to direct his career. Though the executive in this situation is able to avoid the confusion and disorientation experienced by those who are terminated and thus "forced" to become self-directed, individuals who start becoming self-directed while still in secure positions often go through wrenching experiences trying to merge their desired goals with a new career path. Allen Grossman is a case in point. A graduate of Wharton and the current CEO of Outward Bound, Grossman reached the height of his commercial career in 1980, but it took nine full years of searching before he decided where he wanted his next career to be. After fifteen years of running a family-owned national paper and packaging company, Grossman realized, "I had to go to the next plateau in order to continue having fun." He explained:

My interest in sixties social causes reengaged and I decided that I would be more satisfied applying what I knew in a different area that was in the not-for-profit sector.

Grossman's immediate goal was to learn as much as he could about the not-for-profit sector while building a résumé that would eventually enable him to take a salaried position in a not-for-profit organization. He got involved in pro bono work, handled conflict resolution in the Soviet Union and the Middle East, which resulted in an appearance on ABC's *Nightline* news program, and became the managing partner of a group setting up community foundations in Africa and South America. In 1991, when a board member from Outward Bound approached him about becoming CEO, Grossman recalls, "I was forty-six and had never had a job interview. I decided to get experience interviewing." Grossman's nine-year odyssey ended when that "first interview" led to an offer to become Outward Bound's new CEO.

Executives like Allen Grossman seek hands-on experience through pro bono work, volunteering, and consulting stints in order to gain the experience they will need to accomplish a complete career switch. While they avoid the confusion, anger, and disorientation experienced by those who become portable through termination, these executives find their own frustration in working two or more positions simultaneously, and in realizing how long it takes to gain experience and build a reputation in another field.

When You Are the Downsizing Agent

What happens when the directive to downsize the organization lands on your desk? Executives who serve as downsizing agents are the first to witness the immediate effects of dismantling the once-secure lifetime employment system, and are often among the first to realize that even their own positions may not be as secure as they may have imagined. Robert L. Byrne, former in-house counsel for Columbia-Presbyterian Medical Center in New York, explains what it was like to be a downsizing agent:

> **Diamonds are forever; jobs are not. This becomes apparent if you serve as in-house counsel for an employer experiencing "reductions-in-force." Illusions about the permanence of an employment "compact" evaporate pretty quickly when you wield the reorganization scalpel.**

Portable executive Ed Sanford also discovered that job permanence was a thing of the past when carrying out his assignment as a downsizing agent. After accepting an attractive offer from the CEO of a major corporation to head up and "grow" one of its divisions, Sanford quickly realized that the corporate agenda was far different from the long-term opportunity he'd been pitched at his interview. As he began cutting excess inventory and streamlining operations, it became increasingly apparent that the company planned to sell off the division he'd been hired to "grow." When Sanford successfully trimmed the division down to a lean and marketable enterprise, his job was trimmed as well.

While the downsizing agent may have the most warning that he or she will soon be out of a job, the benefit of knowing it's coming is often obviated as downsizing agents are usually busy right up to their last day of employment. For those like Robert L. Byrne, serving as a downsizing agent provides the certain knowledge that the culture of lifetime employment is over, and that they, too, must plan their careers with a portable mind-set.

Time to Take the Next Hill

Many executives move from corporation to corporation in search of greater challenge. Ed Sanford, a former president of Prince Matchabelli, is a case in point.

> I was approaching forty, and I thought, "Do I want to make some changes? If so, then now's the time to do it." So I went to my boss and said, "I'm leaving." It was really that simple.

Robert C. Hall, the current CEO of the Toronto-based Thomson Corporation's Information/Publishing Group, has been a portable executive for his entire career—working at or near the top of a number of different companies in six different industries. "I would get antsy," explains Hall. "I simply could not tolerate a situation where I was not continuously challenged."

Marketing executive Jack Gelman has also been portable most of his life:

> I have never thought of anything as permanent—in the sense of a place where you'd work for twenty years— partly because of my need for constant challenge. I don't perceive any position as lasting beyond five years.

This is not to say, however, that because these individuals choose the moves they make, they do not experience some of the same trauma as those who have been terminated. Robert C. Hall says, "We moved a lot! My daughter never went to the same school two years in a row until she got into the eighth grade. You can't move like I did without a supportive family."

A Retirement That Looked Good on Paper

There are executives as well, who, having taken early retirement with a reasonable amount of contentment and more than adequate severance packages, find themselves either bored or missing life in an organization. Joseph Bevan, a former vice president of personnel and operations for Richardson-Vicks, had given his retirement a great deal of thought. Upon taking his last assignment within Richardson-Vicks, he said, "I'll go out and do this for four years and then I'll retire." Says Bevan:

> I had said, "I'll have no problem sliding into retirement. I have other interests. I'm not hung up on how valuable I've been to this company. I don't define myself by those terms." After retiring and spending a lot of time at home, I was a bit itchy—I was uncomfortable with not doing *anything*. I found myself thinking, "I still have something to say and I believe I can use my experience to help companies deal with difficult situations effectively."

Bevan did not want to return to an organization full-time, so he chose to become a portable executive because it allowed him to work on short, intense business assignments and spend the rest of his time as he pleased.

Though certainly not as traumatic an experience as that of an executive who needs to find a new position for economic reasons, the disorientation and grief an executive in this situation may experience can be every bit as debilitating. After being a part of an organization for years, retired executives are left trying to find work that will be deeply satisfying and engage all of their talents.

In the end, regardless of which of these situations motivates an executive to recognize his or her need to become more self-directed, common to all is the fact that there is no longer an organization to define them, and their dependence on an organization to define their sense of self has come to an end. Former Union Carbide executive Ed Burrell described it this way:

> The longer you work for a large corporation, the more dependent you become on it psychologically and financially. You begin to doubt your ability to support yourself without the company job. This kind of dependency takes away from the self-sufficiency I feel everyone should have. And it's hard to recognize—I didn't sense my dependency when I was at Union Carbide, but once I was outside, I clearly saw what had happened to my self-worth over the years.

Portable executive Michael Hostage, who has served as chairman of the Continental Baking Company, a division of ITT, as well as chairman of the Howard Johnson Company, talked about how he defined himself during the early days of his career at Procter & Gamble:

> As a young man coming out of college, I identified myself by the company I worked for and my title. If you asked me "Who are you?" I would have told you who I worked for and what I did. Today, I own a series of small companies, but I'm not defined by any one of them.

To grow beyond defining oneself by an organization or a title, the executive committed to becoming self-directed needs to break through an ingrained set of habits and roadblocks.

Culture Shock

While the intensity of the anxieties, fears, and practical problems that arise for an individual who has just been downsized varies, almost all people experience a profound degree of culture shock when they no longer work full-time for an organization. The first shock, of course, is that of suddenly being without any income, with the loss of medical benefits—a major part of compensation—a close second.

Also among the initial shocks the individual confronts is the loss of social status he enjoyed within the community. An executive's sense of dignity, power, and self-esteem are not only tied to his position within a corporation, but also to his status in the community. A loss of power is also felt by many executives as they abandon clearly defined positions of authority. Portable executive Jack Cahill says:

> **The power was gone. I didn't realize I even had any power until I didn't have it. The people who used to "pay homage" to me before didn't pay me much attention when they found out I wasn't in that position anymore. I've talked to other people who felt the same thing. You walk into a restaurant, and people say "Hi! Good to see you again. What are you doing?" When you respond, "I left, and I'm really looking for a job," you get a very different feeling from people. It isn't money, because I still had that, but I didn't have the power. It's power that commands respect.**

Many executives serve on the boards of commercial organizations and major charities because they represent the presence of their organization in the community. Often, a newly downsized executive finds himself not only without a job, but asked to step down from the charitable and corporate boards they serve on. When Mike Hostage took early retirement, he soon found that a bank where he served on the board of directors no longer required his services. Hostage's core skills hadn't changed, but the bank's perception of him had, assuming that his value was a result of his affiliation with the organization.

For most executives, the shock of realizing that job loss or early retirement often carries with it a loss of status compounds the concern that if they aren't working they aren't worth much. Though it may sound like a rationalization, it is important to remember that these rejections are just a consequence of the old view that organizations provide individual value and self-worth.

The Sense of Worthlessness

One of Bud Titsworth's first thoughts after being fired from J. Walter Thompson was, "Gee, if I got canned, I must not be very good at what I do. Being fired was a shock to my ego. I had a lot of self-doubts." This feeling reflects the worker's view of himself as a "cog in the wheel" rather than as a critical gear that keeps the organization running. "After a while," says Titsworth, "I realized the problem was between me and the organization I worked for. They didn't perceive me as somebody who was valuable any longer. That didn't mean, though, that I wasn't valuable to someone else. It simply meant that, in their view, they didn't need me." The reality, as Titsworth's reflections suggest, is that no organization can strip an executive of the value of his or her skill set. Mike Hostage explains how he came to see his relationship as an individual executive with the organization he happened to work for: *The definition in the old days would have been, 'I relate to the company,' whereas today, I'd say, 'These activities relate to me.'*

Where Can I Find a Job at My Age?

While age is undeniably a factor as baby boomers compete for the same positions as newly downsized, mid-career managers, the notion of true competition is open for serious analysis. Eck Vollmer, a former CFO of the Gestetner Corporation who has successfully worked as a portable executive for several years, said this of his own no-fault termination:

> **Coming out of Gestetner, I was of an age which made it difficult for me to get hired. But I don't think that younger people are truly in competition with those of us who have been around awhile. They may bring new ideas, but we bring experience. I mean it's one thing to be smart, but unless you've been through a lifeboat drill a couple of times, it's not easy.**

George Balinski, the former director of information systems for Mercedes-Benz of North America, remarked:

> **After a major corporation reorganizes, it is usually left with too few people who know the inner workings of the organization. What you're left with are the young bucks who are usually business-naive.**

While it is often true that younger people are better trained, have more energy, and will work for less compensation, the downsizing of the nation's corporations has left organizations with fewer older, seasoned executives who possess the depth of experience required to mentor the current generation.

The Cash-Flow Crisis

Often, one of the most serious concerns for the newly down-sized executive is the need to generate income. Though early-retirement incentives and "golden parachutes" were often too good to pass up in the early days of downsizing over a decade ago, today, as some corporations enter into their third, fourth, or perhaps fifth wave of major reorganization, those types of packages are shrinking in value and quite a few executives have come away with "parachutes of lesser metal." As restructurings become more commonplace, severance packages will become less attractive for all levels of management.

The anxiety and sudden lack of cash flow may spur an executive to hit the job market immediately and take the first job he or she can get in order to avoid a significant change in lifestyle. Later, these executives often discover that they are part of the growing "bouncing ball" crowd described earlier in this section, because they haven't yet assessed their core competencies or determined their market value and the possible alternative applications of their core skills. Portable CEO Robert C. Hall says: "Don't leap too quickly. First, think about what you want to do and don't make a decision until you don't feel so panicky."

In their initial panic, many executives fail to take the time to assess their situation and develop an organized economic plan. Developing such a plan immediately can greatly reduce the anxiety an executive experiences when initially reviewing his financial resources, as doing so often reveals that he can afford to step back and calmly plan his next career move.

Of course, some executives cannot afford to be out of work for long and do need to take the next available job after they are downsized, but this does not necessarily mean that they will automatically join the bouncing-ball crowd. Portability is a mind-set, and regardless of whether or not an executive takes the first position available to him, he can certainly continue developing the portable mind-set and identifying his core capabilities and the possible market applications for them. For those who must go back to work immediately, it may simply take longer to reach the point where they are making optimal use of their core skills in an environment that also gives them the highest level of personal challenge and satisfaction. In this case, where an executive engages in his searching period while he is employed full-time, it is important to remember that as the executive evolves, the position he creates over time will be increasingly based on the optimal use of his skills.

No Benefits, No Perks

Foremost in the minds of most downsized executives is how to provide the medical coverage for themselves and their families that was once provided by the organization. Technically, medical benefits are a part of compensation and not, as most people tend to think of them, "perks"; COBRA (Consolidated Omnibus Budget Reconciliation Act) laws allow employees to purchase their medical insurance from their former employers for up to eighteen months after termination. Sometimes, however, the cost of doing so sends downsized executives scrambling for more affordable health insurance. Some, like former Gestetner executive Eck Vollmer, have working spouses whose medical benefits will automatically cover them, but many others must begin searching for affordable coverage immediately. Executives in this position should look into industry and other professional organizations they may belong to, as often these groups offer access to group medical, dental, and other benefits at considerably less cost than either individual plans or COBRA plans.

Though not all downsized executives and managers have major perks to lose when they are terminated, it's hard not to feel the loss if you have enjoyed them. The day that George Balinski was downsized out of Mercedes-Benz, for example, he realized he had to turn in the keys to the company car he'd enjoyed while he was employed there.

For many, the loss of a support staff is profoundly disorienting, as some are truly at a loss when faced with handling their own typing, filing, and computer-related needs. Many executives have enjoyed the privilege of having a secretary or assistant, and may not possess even the most basic computer literacy. In order to cope with this loss, the majority of the executives we interviewed made gaining computer literacy a top priority.

There are, of course, "perks" which one can easily live without, though it is understandable that losing them may come as a blow to the ego. As an executive strives to adopt a portable mindset, she must weigh yesterday's perks against the satisfaction, compensation, and quality of life that today's portability affords.

Creating New Habits

While the level and intensity of these various anxieties, practical problems, and fears vary with the individual, all find that they must develop new habits that are more in tune with today's portable lifestyle. Some, like Allen Grossman and Manny Elkind, accomplish their transitions gradually within the organization and don't seem to be as profoundly affected, because they eventually emerge in an environment that they've created for themselves. Others, like Mike Fleming, George Balinski, and Dave Moore, are struck by some form of panic or intense anxiety as soon as they are downsized; while still others who may be initially excited about a new venture realize they have yet to find something that provides them with a high-enough level of personal and professional satisfaction.

One way to approach the anxiety, panic, and disorientation that accompany the period immediately following being downsized is to begin to create new habits. As you do, you will discover that often the old habits themselves are the actual cause of many of the anxieties and fears that accompany this period—you feel that you should be doing something a certain way, because that's the way you always did it while working for a particular organization, or because you think society expects it of you, and as soon as you stop doing something a certain way, or stop doing it altogether, you're flooded with anxiety.

The trick is to begin determining which of the old habits serve you and which do not. Here are some practical suggestions for severing ties with habits that no longer fit, and some techniques to help you allay your anxieties and fears.

- If economics allow, don't go anywhere near an office for a while and don't look for a job. Take time off— longer than your average vacation—and spend part of it at home. You'll discover that there is an entire world that exists outside the office.
- Experience the day-to-day routine of your family. Most likely, you're used to spending most of each day away from your family. You'll be surprised to find out how much goes on while you're at the office.
- Since there is a lot of stress involved in this period of adjustment, practice stress management immediately. Go jogging, ride a bike, work out. The health of your body and the health of your mind are inextricably connected, so remember that reducing stress physically will pay off mentally as well.
- Keep a journal. Scribbling your daily reactions to things and noting your feelings in a journal will help you to manage panic by providing a way to track the patterns of your feelings over time. It will also help you identify those habits you want to break and will aid in establishing new habits that are necessary and important to this phase of your life.
- Become involved in your community through volunteer work and other activities. If you've ever said, "I'd love to coach Little League, if I only had the time," *now* is the time. Help out at a local soup kitchen or women's shelter. Your portable skills are community builders. Use them to help others and savor the personal satisfaction you get from being able to do so.
- Take advantage of all the counseling that's available to you— outplacement, support groups, etc. Losing your job is no longer something to be ashamed of—in fact, it's so common that getting together with others in the same situation can help you to develop perspective and realize that you are not

alone. Groups can offer a camaraderie that can help you recover your good feelings about yourself and prove helpful in generating new ideas and creative approaches to portability.

Former Eastman Kodak executive Chuck Trowbridge offered a good example of how to spend time breaking old habits. "The first thing I did was to start using my hands. I redid the basement. I also set up a schedule for practicing the piano and got into a new exercise program."

The world is changing, and though you may have learned it the hard way, you've got to be prepared to change with it. You are part of an emerging phenomenon in the workplace, which, if understood and dealt with, can have an extremely positive effect on your career and your approach to life. You are breaking old habits and learning new things about yourself. Ultimately, the changes you are making will lead to a better-balanced, more personally satisfying way of living and working, but only if you take the time to make those changes now. Break the habits that no longer serve you, and soon you'll be ready to set your course in the new direction of becoming part of the portable workforce.

Chapter Five

ASSESSING YOUR

PORTABLE SKILLS

◆

**If you're in a situation like I was, where you end up tak-
ing a hike, you say "Okay, now what?" and what it forces
you to do is really take stock of your skills and say,
"Okay, where can I apply these skills and enjoy applying
them, and can I make money doing it?" It sounds wacky
to say this, but properly perceived, being out of work
can be the best thing that ever happened to you.**

—Richard Borel

As the emerging portable executive comes to grips with the
shifts in the marketplace and accepts the idea that the only real
career success depends on operating as a "personal service business entity," the process of evaluating his or her skills and determining which of them have the greatest value in the marketplace
begins in earnest. The standard approach recommended for executives undertaking a job search is to honestly evaluate both their
skills and what they like to do. This usually results in a clear focus on those skills that have been the most effective in the past
and a reaffirmation of the kind of job the executive is looking for.
While the process described in this chapter may be similar to the

one followed in a standard job search, the idea is that in order to make the core attitudinal shift to self-direction and thereby portability, the search and evaluation process for a portable executive must be much broader and more intense than that undertaken in a traditional job search and skill evaluation.

During this searching period, portable executives must come to understand themselves as "personal service business entities" rather than "employees of business entities." This is true even if they have already taken a short-term position to generate cash flow, or think that they would one day like to return to work for a large organization. The individual will learn, as he or she passes through the searching period, that employers today are simply vehicles through which portable executives deliver their skills. Every executive must be prepared for a marketplace where work assignments last finite, predetermined periods of time and individuals take full charge of their own career paths. To arrive at this new view of the relationship between an organization and an executive, individuals need to reconsider their attitude about themselves and those they work for.

Valuing Your Skills

Long-term employees often fail to recognize the value of their skills outside of the context of the organization they work for. Portable executives, on the other hand, perceive their skills as valuable assets that belong to them and are separate and distinct from the organizations they are currently servicing. While it may be relatively easy to accept this shift in attitude intellectually, the actual process involved requires a reevaluation of one's self-confidence, one's need for security, and one's risk orientation. This reevaluation gives emerging portable executives an opportunity to explore other applications of their skills that they might not have considered while working for their long-term employer. When Ed Burrell evaluated his own skill set, for example, he discovered he could take the chemical and treasury experience he developed while with Union Carbide and create a consulting and investment-banking boutique that focused on the chemical industry.

Relations with the Organization

The second attitudinal shift portable executives need to make is toward the relationships within the organizations they have worked for and those they will work for in the future. This is the shift from viewing oneself as an "employee of a business entity" to one of being an independent "personal service business entity," and while this shift may be subtle, it involves accepting the idea that one will work for multiple employers throughout a career, and that work on the basis of short-term projects will be a routine part of doing business and a way of life. Portable executive Sam Marks says:

> **I think there is even a criteria for ending a short-term assignment. The first part of completing an assignment as a portable executive is that whatever you agreed to do is now over. You walk away saying, "I've been paid a fee," and the CEO or whoever is rating you says that you either have or have not accomplished what you were supposed to do.**

During this period of adjustment, portable executives must wrestle not only with the loneliness of working alone or in small groups, but also with the additional responsibilities of running their business, a task once handled by their employers.

Probably one of the more significant shifts in attitude concerning relations with organizations and those within them is that the portable executives seek cooperative, rather than competitive, relationships with those they work with. This is a result of the fact that the content of the work and completion of the task assigned are their primary motivators, rather than, as in organizational settings, rank, title, or status.

Measurement of Success

As portable executives move toward self-direction, they must reexamine their definition of "success," which can initially be very troubling. The portable executive must first see herself as independent of any organization she is currently servicing. Then she must come to see that success is not measured by the organization, but is based on the quality of the job done and the results the portable executive actually attains. It is no longer enough for an executive to satisfy the organization she is servicing; she must now satisfy the standards of quality she has set for herself. Adopting a set of self-imposed quality standards may require a significant shift in attitude.

Financial Security

Operating as an independent portable executive often introduces a lack of predictability in terms of income and cash flow, as well as a need to invest funds in maintaining the portable executive's most critical assets—his or her skills. For many executives, the adjustment from the certainty of receiving a reliable paycheck to the uncertainty of waiting for clients to pay their fees (as well as not always knowing exactly when a particular client relationship will end) is a critical factor in becoming portable. Bud Titsworth speaks for the majority of portable executives when he says:

> I had grown up professionally being in places where money arrived on a regular basis. I thought about money in terms of how much I made, whether I was going to get a raise, and what the bonus would be. Now there are times when it's real busy and money is coming in and

times when it's not real busy and there isn't any money coming in. That's when I have to ask myself, "What can I do to generate revenue?"

The Searching Period

While long-term employers may have made life easier by assessing an executive's capabilities and utilizing them to the best advantage of the organization, that does not necessarily mean that the organization utilized all of an executive's core skills or even those in which he or she possessed the most expertise. As executives undertake the process of formally assessing their own skills, they often find areas to which they are particularly attracted, but which they have never used in business.

Now that the organization is no longer there to set the parameters for the executive, as Richard Borel points out, the opportunity for the executive to assess his or her own skills and interests can be very exciting. For many executives, this searching period is a time that allows them to match their passions—what they want most to do in their careers—with core skills they may have underutilized in previous positions.

Dealing with Risk and Ambiguity

As I've gotten older, I've become much more risk-tolerant, for reasons that have nothing to do with economics. Life is short. If you don't do things that provide excitement and fulfillment, you just hate yourself later on. It's like Cher says: "Life is not a dress rehearsal." It's your only chance.

—Stuart Litt

One of the benefits of working within a large organization is that, even during the upheaval of a downsizing, executives can assess the apparent risks to themselves fairly easily. As one moves toward becoming a portable executive, however, the question of risk orientation becomes much more significant and a new factor of ambiguity is added. The emerging portable executive must work hard to assess the difference between real risk, be it financial or emotional, and the feelings of ambiguity that naturally accompany adopting new approaches. For example, investing in a start-up company may involve real financial risk, while working for multiple employers may involve dealing with ambiguous feelings toward work. The poet John Keats wrote:

> **At once it struck me what quality went to form a man of achievement . . . negative capability . . . that is when a man is capable of being in uncertainties, mysteries, doubts. . . .**

While the searching period is certainly characterized by "uncertainties, mysteries, and doubts," creating one's own path through and beyond them is at the core of the process of becoming a portable executive. Some individuals need the security and consistency offered by being a member of a large group, while others thrive working alone. Portable executives must assess their own tolerance for risk in order to assure that they achieve career success in light of the goals that they choose for themselves.

All relationships involve risk and ambiguities. The important thing for the searching portable executive is to seek to understand his own personal comfort zones, and to remember that the process of searching is one that is continuous in nature and does not end once the portable executive chooses an initial direction. He must continue the process throughout his career. Portable executives constantly review the applicability of their skills in the marketplace, developing relations with new and existing clients and monitoring the quality of their offerings. As Richard Borel puts it:

The process of searching never stops. It's something you go through daily—the self-evaluation—it's a kind of weeding process and it's painful sometimes, but if you can look at situations that seem negative and change them into positive ones, then this process becomes very easy.

Developing Guidelines

Just as the parameters set for executives by large organizations freed them to concentrate on their work, developing a disciplined approach to the searching period will free portable executives from some of the anxieties that accompany this process by providing them with a way to measure their progress. Without a plan, we all tend to drift. Former human resources executive Wayne Thurston says, "I try to plan my activities weekly whether they be physical activities—which I've increased tremendously—or work activities." Following are general guidelines for incorporating a disciplined freedom into the searching period. It is important to emphasize, however, that each portable executive will undoubtedly tailor the guidelines to create an individual approach that enables him or her to achieve the attitudinal changes necessary for career success.

The process of searching entails collecting information and entertaining the idea of pursuing various avenues. Keep a list of the areas you want to explore, people you wish to talk to, and the progressive results of your search, so you can see how the various elements and activities relate to one another. Portable executive Richard Achilles advises:

Don't be too confined in your assessment and appraisal of your own capabilities. Once you have decided what kind of work you want to do, write it down. Don't just try to speak it, even though that's important.

Writing down the various information gained during the search period provides you, the portable executive, with a ready record of what has worked for you and what hasn't. Since you will be pursuing a number of options and ideas at once, creating this written record will allow you to easily see where the results of your search are leading. The act of writing also helps you identify the possible connections between ideas for work alternatives that you may not have seen before.

- SETTING A TIME PARAMETER

Time parameters should be flexible and somewhat open-ended—for example, three to six months—and shouldn't function to place undue restrictions on you, but simply help you to pace the activities you engage in. Any process that is designed to create change within an individual cannot be limited by a strict time frame, but being aware of time helps the searching executive to remain focused.

- PERSONAL FINANCIAL SITUATION

Evaluate and include your personal financial position as part of the overall searching process, as financial considerations will definitely influence the choices you examine and eventually make. It is critical for portable executives to have a good grasp of their personal financial situation so they may realistically gauge how much time and money they can invest in developing a self-directed career. The realities of one's financial situation serve as a true starting point in examining one's tolerance for risk.

- ESTABLISHING A PLACE TO WORK

If you are not currently working on an assignment, or do not have the use of an office through an outplacement service, allocate some portion of your home for workspace. This area should be reserved for the purpose of your work only. Waiting until the kitchen table is free will only throw a disciplined approach off track. Then, too, from a psychological point of view, since the searching period is often fraught with anxiety, you should establish a workplace for yourself where you feel comfortable and relaxed.

- SCHEDULING ACTIVITIES

Create a schedule for your activities. While your schedule will be influenced by whether or not you are currently working full-time, it is still important to allocate set times on the weekends or in the evenings for meeting the goals of your search. If you are not working, this schedule should include time for activities not strictly related to work, such as exercise, getting involved in community affairs, attending a support group, and meeting with business and other contacts to avoid becoming too isolated. The built-in camaraderie that comes with working in a large organization every day is something most executives find they miss. It is important to establish regular times for meeting with other people to offset the isolation of working on your own. This is part of the process of creating new habits for yourself, and it is important that in making the shift to viewing yourself as a business that you provide for the need for camaraderie as well.

- RESOURCES

Formal processes such as receiving outplacement counseling, joining support groups, doing research, or arranging to meet new people are all resources that need to be planned for during the searching period. Much of this resource identification has to be done by you yourself, which will lead you to rediscover the public library, learn about databases, and possibly interact with church groups you never would have been involved with before. Finding these resources is an exercise that will help stand you in good stead as you strike out on your own.

- TESTING

Finally, as you evaluate your skills, make sure to allot sufficient time to test them in the marketplace. There are many ways to measure the realistic applications of the skills you are exploring.

It can be done through networking, taking short-term consulting assignments, or applying the skills you want to test in a volunteer activity in your community.

Taking Inventory

Whether you are involved in a formal outplacement program, are spending weekends and evenings at home thinking about your evolution as a portable executive while currently holding a job, or are in some other way engaging in the searching process on your own, you must first undertake some focused exercises that will enable you to evaluate your attitudes and skills and allow you to explore new avenues or approaches. There are many different techniques available for doing this, and alternative methods can be found in career books available in any local library, through outplacement counseling, job seminars at church and community centers, and networking with friends who have been through the experience.

Regardless of how you approach this evaluation, you will want to adopt some type of standard measure that you can use throughout your career. Unlike the organizational snapshot assessment of your skills and attributes, this process should launch you into a mode of continuous evaluation. During the searching period, you will be processing an unusually large amount of information and getting to know yourself on a deep level. It is therefore a good idea to practice and evaluate these exercises on a daily basis; but at a very minimum, you should do them at least once a week, and keep track of the shifts that occur as time goes by. What will emerge is a clearer picture of how best to apply your core skills in a self-directed manner.

Assessing Your Attributes and Capabilities

Divide a piece of paper into two columns and list on one side your attributes—those things that come naturally to you and which you like to do—and on the other side your capabilities—

the skills that you have acquired. Do not restrict the items on these lists to attributes and capabilities employed in work situations, but rather broaden it to include your entire life. We are all born with certain inherent attributes that we do not always recognize as having value and thus may have never applied them in our work lives. After he took early retirement from Xerox, Bob Kane identified the deep desire to serve others that had been instilled in him from his early Jesuit training. "After a mix of community assignments and volunteer work," says Kane, "I recognized my deep desire to serve mankind." He combined his natural attribute of wanting to serve mankind with his business capabilities, and took on an assignment in the Third World for the International Executive Services Corps.

Over the course of a lifetime, we acquire certain capabilities that make us "expert" in certain areas, but we may not necessarily have taken advantage of all of these attributes. The result of Bob Kane's search was a better attribute-capability match that offered him greater personal fulfillment than he initially had after early retirement.

Perhaps the most important part of this exercise is to focus considerable attention on those areas that you have underutilized or never employed in a formal work situation, as these attributes and capabilities often yield fresh clues as to the direction your career could take. As we saw with Manny Elkind, after working in production and manufacturing at Polaroid for the majority of his career and making only limited use of his skills as a teacher, his new business sprang from a decision to follow, as he put it:

My own instinct about where my satisfaction was. That's when I changed careers and in effect made my avocation my vocation.

Elkind took his previously untapped talent for teaching others, coupled it with his newfound passion for understanding how people cope with change, and from that match built a business. This is something that can only be done when an executive has a thorough awareness of his or her attributes and capabilities and how to make the most of them.

Over time, as you list your capabilities and attributes, you should begin to rank them in terms of strength. Again, you may find that capabilities and attributes previously undervalued, or which need further development, will offer the greatest reward in the marketplace. Over a period of time, your attribute-capability matches will become more readily apparent, and the areas in which you are best suited to work will emerge.

Aligning Your Career Path with Your Passions

While the previous exercise measures your natural and acquired skills, this exercise will help you weigh what you are really good at against what you really enjoy. Once again, divide a piece of paper in half. On one side list everything that you're good at; on the other, everything you like to do. At first, you may not see much that seems compatible, but as you spend more time talking to other people, making notes, exploring other businesses and industries and doing informal research, the items that fill those lists are likely to change considerably.

At the outset of his own search, John Thompson never believed he belonged in the human resources business and, in fact, turned down several opportunities to join search firms. But as his own search progressed, what emerged was a very clear match between his attributes and capabilities and what he enjoyed doing and was good at. The results led him to create his own unique "search" firm.

No searching process would be complete without testing your ideas about where to take your career against the backdrop of the real world. Over a period of time, these lists will grow shorter as you assess their practicality. For instance, if you've always wanted to play professional hockey, but are fifty-five years old, you should probably remove that from your list and coach peewee hockey for personal fulfillment. These exercises should be done over and over again as you obtain more information and discover new opportunities in the marketplace. As you fine-tune these lists, you are getting ready to take the next step in the process: searching and networking in your areas of interest.

Evaluating the Way You Make Choices

One of the hardest adjustments you need to make in moving toward portability is the recognition that you have the ability to choose the kind of career or work that you like to do. If you ask people why they aren't doing what they'd like to do, you usually get the impression—either directly or indirectly—that they don't believe they have any choice in selecting a career. In this exercise, you will examine how you go about making choices and gaining a better understanding of their impact. Here are some examples:

- If you are at all interested in the stock market, select two or three stocks listed in the newspaper and keep track of their prices over a period of time to see how you would have done if you had bought them. Obviously, this is a very random-choice process, and you may or may not have success with it. Now do some research on specific stocks and, again, keep track of their prices to see how they compare with your randomly selected stocks. Regardless of how "well" you do, you will notice that since you have more information about them you are more comfortable and assured that you made a reasonable choice. The point of this random-versus-thoughtful-choice exercise is to help you understand that the more you know, the more you can cut down your risk of making a bad choice.
- If, as part of your reorientation or adjustment period, you have chosen to maintain an exercise program, keep track of the progress you make—distances run, laps swum, or weights lifted. This will illustrate objectively how a choice to under-

take a disciplined activity results in measurable change.

- Observe the number of choices you make during a given time period, such as half a day, and then consider any patterns that emerge, such as a tendency to tackle the hard things first or a tendency to procrastinate. By acknowledging the ways in which you make choices, you will come to understand how you deal with difficult, and easy, situations.

Envisioning Portability

Some of your time during the searching period should be spent envisioning what life will be like as a portable executive. Try imagining what you will look like as a portable executive, then create visions of what you need to do to get there. It is much like playing tennis or golf, in which you consciously or unconsciously envision what the perfect shot or serve will look like as the benchmark for your actual performance. Obviously, when the perfect shot is made, you get a tremendous feeling of fulfillment, but even if it isn't perfect, you benefit from a sense of how close you were and what improvements can be made to accomplish it.

You should set aside time on a regular basis for envisioning sessions. Sit down, close your eyes, and imagine what you would like to be doing and what you would accomplish doing it. This should be done for a set period of time, like half an hour or forty-five minutes, during which you let your imagination decide what the results might be. If you like, put down what you see in your vision in a drawing or in writing in your journal, or simply keep it in your mind's eye. As you continue envisioning, you will also become aware of the factors that prevent you from achieving this vision. For example, you may envision yourself as a consultant and an individual practitioner but encounter resistance in taking the financial risk of not having a paycheck. This type of information gives you the opportunity to examine your tolerance for financial risk during your searching period and may lead you to a type of job where, for example, you join a larger consulting firm that gives you a moderate amount of working independence and the consistency of a paycheck.

Mapping Your Journey

During the searching period, a plethora of ideas, feelings, hopes, and fears crop up at different times. It is important to capture these ideas and feelings to guide you in your searching process, and there is no better way to do this than by keeping a journal. While there are many books that offer specific techniques for journal writing, each person will approach it slightly differently. Basically, journal writing involves writing about what you are doing and what you are thinking about. The important thing is to keep a notebook handy and enter your feelings, ideas, thoughts, and observations into it on a regular basis. Your journal should be private, to be shared with no one, so you should feel comfortable including your deepest feelings and fears. Your observations about choices, your capabilities and attributes lists, as well as your visions can all be part of your journal, along with your observations about the day, meetings, and information you turn up in your research. In addition, and probably most important, include your "crazy" ideas in the journal. Things that at first don't make any sense over time may reveal patterns in your life and things about yourself and your interests that you hadn't discovered before.

Keeping a journal will allow you to review your thoughts conveniently, and may prove to be an invaluable source of new insight into what you really want to do.

Collecting Information

A major portion of the searching period will be devoted to collecting information. It is in this stage of the searching period that a critical part of becoming a portable executive kicks in—adopting a spirit of cooperation through an appreciation of the unique capability and skill sets of other people. As the emerging portable executive begins to engage in information collection, he or she quickly discovers that people they didn't have much use for while operating within large organizations often have tremendous amounts of knowledge that will help them examine their choices. As Ken Heimberg of AT&T put it:

> **Networking is most productive when you have a reason to meet with people. If you find an area of interest, a specific subject or theme in networking and discuss it, you exchange value and people start to open up. I learned that everybody has some major things to contribute and it's very important not to make value judgments about people, but to really listen to them because some people will really surprise you with the contribution they will make.**

As the portable executive goes about collecting information, perhaps the most important thing he or she can do is to always bear in mind that everyone has something to offer. One way to open your mind during the searching process is to get involved with brainstorming groups.

With the sheer numbers of downsized executives around these days, it is easy to either find or start your own brainstorming group. Many already exist as part of outplacement counseling programs, through local churches and community groups, and they offer excellent opportunities to open yourself to new ideas, test your thinking about your skills and capabilities, and explore the viability of your choices. On-line computer roundtables, as mentioned before, are also potential sources for locating existing brainstorming groups or beginning one specific to the area you're interested in.

As part of his outplacement experience with Wright Associates, Wayne Thurston attended a weekly brainstorming group in which he and others weighed "what worked and what didn't" in the searching process. Once again, it is helpful to remember to approach these activities with an open mind and to listen intently to how other people are handling the searching process.

Information at Your Fingertips

The emergence of sophisticated databases available at the touch of a computer key provides a tremendous tool for the portable executive who is seeking new ideas. You can become an instant expert on practically any subject through the use of databases, bulletin boards, and on-line networking capabilities that give you access to libraries throughout the world and to almost every major international publication.

Most on-line services offer you the opportunity to either join or start a "roundtable discussion" on just about any issue that attracts you, and these services offer the advantage of allowing you to network on an informal basis with people from all over the globe.

Testing Your Value

Within a large organization, it is often difficult to separate your personal value from that of the organization you work for. For this reason, as emerging portable executives deepen their understanding of themselves as business entities, an important part of the searching process is to test their individual value in the marketplace. One way to begin to see your value apart from the organization is to undertake a project in which you can directly affect the outcome of the activity. Many portable executives engage in volunteer work to test their capabilities. Whether this takes a simple form, such as coaching Little League, where you can observe actual changes in the players over the course of a season, or evolves while working on a community housing project or a shelter, volunteer activities offer ample opportunities to test the value of your new direction and skills.

While portable executives are constantly engaged in a searching mode throughout their lives, this initial transitional searching will eventually evolve into a fairly clear picture of where they want to go and the approach they need to take to get there. The obstacles they will have to overcome will also surface to be dealt with. Portable executives' sense of the value of their skill sets, how they want to work with an organization, the measures of success they arrive at, and their tolerance for financial risk all come together and can be applied to something they really like to do. As we have seen, portable executives emerge from the initial searching process not with a wish list, but with a considered vision of what they have to do and the choices they need to make to attain an integrated work situation. They deal realistically with the obstacles, both external and internal, that they will have to overcome to achieve their vision, and they emerge ready to go forward to create their own jobs.

Chapter Six

INVENTING YOUR BUSINESS

◆

To create what you must is not a matter of choice, but to create what doesn't have to be created is truly precious.
—Robert Fritz, *Creating*

Searching for and inventing a personal service business entity are not separate and distinct activities; rather, they are processes that evolve in relation to each other. As the portable executive deepens her ability to match what she likes to do and wants to do with her core capabilities, a subtle, critical shift occurs. The evolving portable executive begins to move away from the view that "My work is my life" to adopt the more holistic attitude of "My life is my work." With "life" as the central focus, the executive will come to appreciate the real value she offers in the marketplace and the potential applications of her capabilities. Taking this holistic view of oneself is a critical first step in emerging as a personal service business entity.

As you'll see from the following chart, the shift from dependency to self-direction results in a substantially different set of beliefs, leading to a new perspective on one's career and employer.

DEPENDENCY VERSUS SELF-DIRECTION

DEPENDENT	SELF-DIRECTED
1. Self-worth is derived from the organization.	1. Self-worth is inherent in one's core skills and therefore independent of any organization.
2. Economic risk is borne by the organization.	2. The portable executive assumes the economic risk.
3. Loyalty is based on the organization's offer of job security	3. Loyalty is based on the alignment of one's own ideals.
4. Success is measured by status, rank, and recognition from the organization.	4. Success is measured by substantive accomplishments.
5. The executive performs best when a clearly defined set of responsibilities are laid out by the organization.	5. The executive performs best when a passion for doing something is successfully matched with core capabilities.

Stepping-Stones

Regardless of when these attitudinal shifts occur in one's career, they invariably form a foundation upon which the soon-to-become portable executive creates her own job. From this perspective, the portable executive comes to view her employer as a vehicle that enables her to gainfully employ her skills at the highest level, regardless of whether she is working on an interim basis for a short period of time or on a long-term project for one organization. The executive learns to focus on the content of the assignment, consistently doing useful work and building value regardless of whether she is compensated or is working as a volunteer.

The portable executive views each new assignment as a stepping-stone to improving her skill base and, as part of this commitment to constant learning, evaluates potential assignments or jobs in terms of what learning opportunities they offer and whether they will increase her qualifications for future assignments.

Thus, each step along the portable executive's career path is both rewarding and helps to lay the foundation for the next step. Michaelita Quinn has taken a stepping-stone approach throughout her career. While she sensed early on that she had the talent for running a company, she approached each new position as a learning experience and a testing ground for her capabilities.

Quinn, who once held management positions on the nonprofit side of educational organizations, first recognized that she was better suited for the fast-paced, results-oriented for-profit community. To pursue her goal, her next job involved starting and managing a profit center for a for-profit education company that was opening in a number of major markets:

> The company I worked for had an excellent training program, and I was on a steep learning curve. I captured the business end of the business—particularly the marketing and sales area. I put all of these new principles into practice and competed successfully.

While there, Quinn was recruited by a competitor to become a corporate vice president. "For me," says Quinn, "that was the first step in expanding my scope and professional level." Over the next four years, she managed that company's field operations, human resources department, purchasing, and capital expenditures. Quinn then searched for and found a company that would offer her the opportunity to advance to the next level of responsibility in the management structure—that of executive vice president and chief operating officer. These moves were all made to increase her knowledge and responsibility as she moved toward her goal of becoming president of a company.

Quinn's step-by-step process enabled her to continually expand her core capabilities to the point that she reached her goal and became president and COO of Stanley H. Kaplan Educational Center, Ltd., an $80-million subsidiary of the Washington Post Company. Armed with this wealth of experience, Quinn then started her own company, which specializes in business consulting to companies, colleges, and entrepreneurs. Quinn's story amply illustrates the advantages of operating with a portable executive mind-set: She carried her accumulated skills from one position to the next, in each instance adding specific experience that allowed her to advance to the next level. Those who become comfortable and successful as portable executives often engage in a continuous process of merging what they like to do with what they want to do in their work lives and use the stepping-stone method, as Quinn did, to realize their vision of themselves as self-directed business entities.

While each executive evolves differently, as seen in the previous chapter's discussion of the searching period, a common process eventually emerges—one of evaluating past experiences in terms of one's attributes and core capabilities and recombining those elements to meet the demands of the current marketplace. Executives often extend this process through some form of experimentation, which allows them to test these new combinations in developing a new, rewarding, fulfilling career. Allen Grossman's tryout period included numerous and varied assignments—working in the not-for-profit sector on a pro bono basis—in order to add to his demonstrable skill set before interviewing for and getting a permanent position in the not-for-profit sector nine years later.

A Job Is Just a Vehicle

In the absence of lifetime employment commitments, the portable executive approaches his employer as a delivery system for his products or services. Consequently, the type of employment relationship he chooses should offer the most efficient vehicle to bring his capabilities to the market. Portable marketing executive Loren Smith, for example, shifted back and forth between working as a consultant and working for large organizations as the need to leverage his business expanded and contracted. While some of the possible employment relationships a portable executive may enter into are influenced by personal style, ultimately it is this need to find his optimal vehicle that determines a portable executive's final career choice. As the following review of available employment relationship options demonstrates, many vehicles exist, and each has its own distinct advantages and disadvantages. A good way to analyze the alternatives is to rate them against one's personal tolerance for the following:

INDEPENDENCE   Are you comfortable working alone? Do you enjoy freedom and offer a unique service? Are you good at networking and marketing?

SUPPORT   Do you feel a strong need to belong to a community? Do your skills, to be effective, require both human and financial capital? Are you uncomfortable with personal marketing, and do you prefer a structured environment?

RISK   Are you willing to accept uncertainty and the possibility of failure? Are you oriented to long-term payoff? And do you seek high reward?

SAFETY   Do you crave consistency? Do you tend to focus on short-term payoff, and have a low tolerance for failure?

We have rated each of the following employment vehicles based upon our interviews with a hundred portable executives. However, each portable executive must evaluate this criteria for himself.

Going Solo

Working completely alone is probably the hardest way to be a portable executive. The solo practitioner is required to do everything himself, from developing the service and the marketing, to the accounting and office support work, to delivering the product or service. Beyond the obvious disadvantage of spending one's time on non-core-skill-related activities, practicing solo can be self-limiting because, as individuals, we have only a certain amount of capacity. There are only so many hours in a day to service clients and attend to the daily tasks of running a business, such as administrative work and bookkeeping. Solo practice probably lends itself best to a creative skill such as commercial art, writing, decorating, or personal counseling. For example, Frank Gilabert, an early-retired executive from Hattori Seiko, works alone creating books for high school students about how business works.

As more and more services become available at reasonable prices, the ability of the sole practitioner to expand his individual capacity becomes much more economically feasible. Tremendous technological advances—such as software programs to handle accounting, word processing, and desktop publishing, as well as time management and basic legal forms—can be effectively utilized to relieve the pressure on solo portable executives and greatly enhance their capacity.

RATINGS

Independence:	High
Support:	Low
Risk:	Medium
Safety:	Low

Strategic Alliances

Strategic alliances offer portable executives a way to maintain their independence and expand their capability to service a broader market. These relationships involve formal or informal arrangements with other portable executives with complementary skills and ability. Paul Upham, a former senior vice president of human resources for Dun & Bradstreet's Donnelley Marketing, has fostered an informal strategic alliance with another executive to increase his sales capacity:

> **I've set up an informal partnership with a fellow in New York who handles the sales. Basically, he knocks on the doors and I come in and do the close. We have an agreement based on the standards of our business: We do the highest-quality work we can and strive to build long-term relationships. That's the way to build a business.**

The key to forming strategic alliances is to build a relationship in which the core skills of each executive enhances those of the other and brings added value to both parties. Usually, these alliances develop when an executive recognizes the need to expand his services. In these arrangements, each portable executive handles his own expenses and revenues are shared. One positive aspect of the strategic alliance is that it can be formed or disbanded as the need arises, thus offering complete flexibility in expanding and reducing an executive's capacity on an as-needed basis.

RATINGS

Independence:	High
Support:	Low
Risk:	Medium
Safety:	Low

Niche Businesses

You can also create your own business by finding a market niche that your skills and services address and become an expert in that particular area. As Joe Cullen said, "A lot of people are knowledgeable about many things, but do not know much about any given thing." Operating from that wisdom, Cullen focused his efforts on becoming the expert on warehousing when no one else around him possessed more than a smattering of knowledge in that area. When Bob Hallam retired as vice-chairman of development at the Marketing Corporation of America, he and his wife created a unique niche business. They recognized that under the Americans with Disabilities Act, all companies have to change their signage to accommodate people with various disabilities. The legislation requires signs with raised letters, braille, appropriate tint or coloring, and contrasting backgrounds. Bob and his wife went to school and learned about the requirements of Title 3 of the Disabilities Act and became, in effect, experts in the signage requirements. They then contracted with a sign company in Florida to supply them with any signs for which they had orders. They approached various trade associations and became the preferred supplier to their members, mainly on the strength of their knowledge of the requirements.

The Hallams identified an unmet need in the marketplace and set out to fill it. As experts, they supplied the sign company and its clients with what is required under the Americans with Disabilities Act. They made a positive contribution to society, making the world more accessible to those with disabilities, and made a profit doing it.

One of the advantages of becoming a niche player or a portable expert is that, with only a modest amount of marketing and networking on your part, people will seek your services. It also opens up a definable market among users of a particular service or skill in the niche. Becoming a niche player enables solo portable executives to focus their limited resources on a highly defined target market.

RATINGS

Independence:	High
Support:	Low
Risk:	Medium
Safety:	Low

Consulting Firms

Certain types of consulting services can be delivered by large organizations that offer a broad base of talent. Information systems, for example, require four or five different subdisciplines in order to provide full services to the client. As employment arrangements go, consulting firms are more formal than strategic alliances, as the consulting firm requires consistent service quality standards, and working together as a team. A portable executive who chooses this type of employment arrangement can satisfy the desire to have multiple assignments while working for one company either as an employee of the firm or being on contract with one. Consulting firms are advantageous in that they handle the marketing aspects of the business, thus freeing the portable executive to focus more on the technical applications of his or her core skills.

Portable executives who choose this vehicle should be aware that most consulting firms put a good deal of emphasis on business development. If you are hired for your technical skills, longevity often depends on your marketing capability. As Joe Bevan put it:

Half of what you bring is expertise and half is potential business. If you can't offer both, you aren't anywhere near as interesting to people.

RATINGS

Independence:	Medium
Support:	High
Risk:	Low
Safety:	Medium

Starting a Company

The primary reason portable executives start their own companies is that the nature of their product or service requires an organization to deliver it to the customer or client. Marketing executive Ed Sanford created his own company because:

> **I was pretty successful in both a marketing company and a service company that provided products and services. I concluded that I could handle both sides of the equation, so I raised some money and decided to try to do it on my own.**

Such companies often evolve out of successful solo operations. For example, when John Trost reached the limit of his capacity as an individual market researcher, he created a company that eventually consisted of twenty-five professionals. Of course, the disadvantages of starting your own company are that it entails a much broader set of skills and includes handling the responsibilities of administration, marketing, finance, and raising capital.

One approach that can reduce the risks of starting your own business is to spin off from an existing business that you have been involved with within a company, such as Manny Elkind did at Polaroid. Former Union Carbide executive Frank Purcell also entered into a somewhat similar arrangement when he was asked to work for a family-owned importing business. Purcell's goal was to start his own business, so the offer to work full-time did not appeal to him until he and the owner of the business came up with an arrangement that satisfied both their needs. The deal allowed the business owner to get the help he needed in exchange for giving Purcell access to the company's international network. This arrangement offers the advantage of calling on your employer for help either directly or indirectly during the initial phases of start-up.

RATINGS

Independence:	Medium
Support:	Medium
Risk:	High
Safety:	Low

New Ventures

Portable executives often team up with venture capital companies to bring management expertise to start-up companies. This is an appealing option for the portable executive who is an entrepreneur at heart but lacks capital, as there are many venture companies that start with a good idea but need the type of business expertise a portable executive can provide to make it successful. Most of these arrangements offer a modest current compensation schedule and a big success package in the form of stock options and bonuses.

At Xerox Technology Ventures in California, CEO Bob Adams uses interim executives during the start-up period when no one knows whether an enterprise will live or die. Using portable executives allows him the best of both worlds. He attracts top management for the short-term and many will stay on if the venture takes off.

RATINGS

Independence:	Medium
Support:	Low
Risk:	Medium
Safety:	Low

Acquiring a Company

This option is often pursued by executives who have "run companies" for larger organizations and seek the challenges and rewards for themselves. The portable executive who chooses this option must recognize that the forms of support, such as capital and marketing, that he enjoyed while working for a large organization become his responsibility. Portable executive Mike Hostage, who today runs four businesses in partnership with his children and other family members, had considerable experience running companies for ITT, the Howard Johnson Company, and Marriott, but even he was surprised by some of the aspects of running his own companies:

> It took me a year to learn what "profit" really means. Profit in a big company is what the accounting department tells you you've made at the end of the period. Profit in small business is how much is left in the till after you've paid your bills. I may be in the minority, but that was not an easy lesson for me to learn.

A lower-risk way to go about acquiring a company is to go to work for the organization, and then acquire it. This gives the portable executive time to assess the pros and cons of running a company while still not being 100 percent responsible for it.

RATINGS

Independence:	Low
Support:	Medium
Risk:	High
Safety:	Low

Franchises

Owning a franchise has the trappings of ownership while the portable executive really functions as an agent or an arm of a larger organization. In exchange for administrative and product support, the larger organization dictates how you are going to do business. While the franchise relationship is presented in terms of ownership, it usually depends on the franchisor, who can adjust the cost of the product or service and support, and thus control the franchisee's earnings. For this reason, the franchise option requires meticulous due diligence and considerable thought, investigation, and research.

In an article published in the *Harvard Business Review* entitled "The Reluctant Entrepreneur" (1992) Ken Veit wrote a cautionary tale about his own experiences as a franchisee. Initially, Veit, who had bought and sold a number of insurance businesses, chose franchising over buying an existing business, because he knew that "buying someone else's problems is extremely risky. In franchising," wrote Veit, "I could benefit from—rather than pay for—the earlier mistakes of others. But when he learned that Cartoon Corner had negotiated his lease on such favorable terms that the leaseholder was paying for 100 percent of the leasehold improvements, Veit said "every red light in my internal warning system went on." Eventually, Veit watched Cartoon Corner announce it was going into liquidation, and in the end, said Veit, "My sunk costs were more than $100,000." Though Veit's story only portrays his own experience as a franchisee, it serves to underscore the necessity of knowing what you are getting into in choosing franchising as a vehicle.

RATINGS

Independence:	Medium
Support:	High
Risk:	Medium
Safety:	Medium

Going Back to Work for a Large Organization

While this is the alternative many executives pursue, the key to returning to a large organization is to reenter that atmosphere with a portable state of mind. Thus, the portable executive electing this option does not approach the organization with the hope for lifetime security, but with the attitude that this is simply the next step on one's career path. It is important to keep this distinction in mind, as in many instances, what you do in a large organization is dictated by being a part of it. Some portable executives, like Lawrence Smith, move back and forth between consulting and working for large organizations. Citibank had already been a client of Smith's for four years when it offered him a full-time position:

> **It came right at a time when I needed a lot of marketing initiative to compete with the biggest businesses in New York. I was tired of traveling. I had worked with the people at Citibank for about four years, so I already knew them well. It was easy to move back in.**

Today, Smith is consulting again, but the years he spent on staff at Citibank offered him the opportunity to further expand and grow.

RATINGS

Independence:	Low
Support:	High
Risk:	Low
Safety:	Medium

Creating a Job with Your Client

Regardless of which employment option a portable executive elects, he or she must be able to develop an assignment in concert with an employer or client. From a practical point of view, a number of elements are involved in this task.

DEFINING THE ASSIGNMENT

At the outset, both the portable executive and the client must clearly define the task, so that both parties know what they expect from each other. This definition must include not only what the portable executive brings to the party, but also what the client or employer brings to it as well. Never take an assignment that does not feel comfortable, and always be sure to carefully evaluate whether or not you are suited to accomplish the defined assignment and possess the necessary core skills to complete it.

Of course, not every assignment will be a perfect fit, but the portable executive must be capable of doing a good job. As outlined in the stepping-stone process of career building thus far, each assignment improves the executive's marketability. It is therefore extremely important to recognize that it is not advisable to choose an assignment where you estimate you have a better than average risk of failure, since in almost every case the portable executive is perceived as being only as good as his or her last assignment.

PERFORMING DUE DILIGENCE

Portable executives should perform a great deal of research on any company, potential partner, or strategic alliance prospect before making a commitment. As for potential clients, one should seek to find out not only how one's skills can be employed, but also whether it is the type of company the portable executive will feel comfortable working with. While defining the assignment, it is important to address and answer questions that might affect one's ability to complete the assignment. As management consultant Beth Pierce says:

> A prospective client may tell you that the company's computer system is functioning smoothly when, in fact, it is not. At the same time, the client will describe a project in which your work product will, to some degree, be dependent on an accurate database, adequate system configuration, and reasonably problem-free application software.

As to joining with others in alliances, one should also be sure to check their references.

TRYOUTS

If you are not sure whether you should enter into a given employment arrangement as you create your business, arrange for a tryout period or consulting stint in which you are expected to accomplish a highly defined task. Open-ended tryouts don't always work, but those that are mutually beneficial—such as Paul Upham's strategic alliance with another executive who handled sales—provide a good way for both sides to come to understand each other before making a long-term business commitment. Flexible recruitment options such as these have been known to lead to long-term positions, but again, the portable executive needs to remain aware that lifetime employment arrangements are an option only for a very small minority of workers today.

Assessing the Career Value of Every Assignment

The portable executive should clearly define for him- or herself what a given assignment or job offers. Will it increase your skill base? Offer an opportunity to apply your skills in a new or different way? Is it a logical step to the next assignment you want to take? And, finally, is it primarily a way to earn money or an assignment that offers growth?

Since the responsibility for career success is always in the hands of the portable executive, considering and answering these questions in advance will help the executive elect assignments that are clearly aligned with their overall career goals and will possibly help the portable executive to avoid moving in the wrong direction.

The searching and business creation process is lifelong. As a portable executive, you will continually expand your core capabilities, and thus constantly expand the challenge of future jobs and assignments. As you reach a more senior position and gain more experience, the nature of your work relationships will change, but the individual process of growing—creating your own job and determining the best matches for your attributes and core skills—never will. And while the internal process of electing to be self-directed offers some frightening considerations, ultimately, self-directed portable executives find they do not miss their former dependency. When Lawrence Smith returned to his own consulting business, he said:

> After I was back into the bureaucracy, I reached a point where I just didn't want to do that anymore. Emotionally, for the last year and a half, I wasn't a happy camper. The environment of conserving, administrating, and refining things that brings out the best of bureaucracy . . . Well, I'm more of a guru. It's stifling. The team effectiveness is diminished. It is a "Simon Says" game in which there is only one Simon. I'm delighted to be back doing what I'm doing.

Once you have adopted an attitude of self-direction, learning to negotiate and accept responsibility for the practical aspects of operating as a portable executive—even within a large organization—is no small task. The next section of this book is dedicated to addressing the practical problems and concerns of being part of our rapidly emerging, flexible workforce.

Chapter Seven

NETWORKING

◆

Keep that old network going or you're going to have to reinvent the wheel.

—Paul Upham

One of the cornerstones in any portable executive's career is an extensive network system. Not a few executives, however, and particularly those who have held long-term positions in major organizations, find themselves wondering, *"What is networking?"*

Learning what networking is and, equally important, what it is not, is a crucial undertaking for all portable executives—whether they are still employed within large organizations or are building their own businesses as solo practitioners, members of consulting groups, or business owners. Simply stated, networking is the process underlying and supporting the portable executive's efforts to create assignments, assess and upgrade skills, develop client relationships, and gain feedback.

Within hierarchical organizations, networking is also known as "the rumor mill," "the grapevine," and yes, "politics" within "corporate culture."

Whatever you call it, networking is a system by which people pass information among themselves informally in order to exchange knowledge and develop a sense of community. In our current marketplace, where knowledge has replaced labor as the prime driver of the economy and is thus the primary asset, networking is the skill that makes or breaks a portable executive's career.

While networking is truly a means of gathering wealth in a culture where wealth is knowledge, it can never be viewed as a one-way street. It draws on the portable executive's spirit of cooperation rather than competition, in which the sharing of information and understanding becomes a way of life that enables people to both perceive each other's value and to use that value for the benefit of the entire network. Defined as such, being part of a network carries with it responsibilities that are much different from those a corporate executive is used to, and places its emphasis on nonhierarchical modes of relating in which all parties in the network are viewed on an equal basis.

The Essence of Networking

Networking is based on the development of mutual understanding and respect. A good networker is someone who listens and calmly waits his turn to share his ideas and what he has to offer. Former vice president of human resources and operations for Richardson-Vicks, Joseph Bevan, put it this way:

> **I've been listening better. Sure, there is a tendency to want to say "This is what I want to offer, now would you please buy it?" but I find myself saying "What do they want?" more and more these days.**

Bevan's words allude to the danger of attempting to network without listening. An executive who comes into a network and immediately starts telling the other members all about himself and his own capabilities will soon find that the network is not very supportive of him and will soon be nonexistent. Listening skills and the ability to understand what another person is saying—both directly and indirectly—about his own needs is essential to successful networking. The essence of successful networking is, in effect, the essence of good salesmanship and offers any portable executive new to "selling himself" a good nonthreatening way to begin doing it.

Striking the right balance between networking and developing "hard leads" can be very tough. Each portable executive must decide how seriously he wants to commit to a network, and an assessment must be made periodically about whether one's time would be better spent somewhere else or in another network. The best way to stay on top of this problem is to be open and honest both with yourself and with those in your network about the commitment you are willing to make and what you expect to get back. If, for instance, your interests lie in the technical aspects of business, such as computer programming or computer analysis, your involvement with a general management network may be minimal—perhaps just enough to keep yourself up to date. In this situation, you may want to become a member of some broad-based organizations but not always contribute. Being honest with the network about the level of support you are willing to give is appropriate, but it is important never to commit to something you know you are not going to do. Along these same lines, it is essential that you not be openly judgmental about a network's value if you are not deeply involved in it.

As opposed to the "What's in it for me?" approach to developing contacts strictly as a means of generating new business, being part of a network involves a commitment to a mutual exchange of ideas and information on an open basis, even though that may put a particular individual at a disadvantage for a time. Participation in a network, as in any other group, encompasses different levels of involvement and ranges from surface exchanges to deeper levels of communication. As the level of networking deepens, so does the commitment to share information, and the portable executive must be sensitive at all times to the depth of the information being offered and the responsibility to reciprocate equally.

Because networking is based on an exchange of knowledge, the portable executive needs to be aware that everything he or she says will likely be shared with others. Therefore, the portable executive must establish basic confidentiality guidelines whenever he or she is faced with the need to share information of a sensitive nature. The guidelines one establishes should address how much one is willing to share in a given network, to what degree one will respect other network members' requests for confidentiality, and how one plans to negotiate assurances of confidentiality prior to sharing information.

Continuing Relationships

Evolving relationships within a network require continuous interaction. A clear understanding of each person's needs and requirements can only be developed over a period of time and through a variety of ways. As with any developing relationship, relationships within a network require a fairly intense "getting to know you" period in which the parties see each other frequently and in various situations. In developing network relationships, it is not sufficient to have lunch once a quarter; rather, projects, mutual interests, and outings should be shared. Ann Rarich speaks of the dangers of letting your network lapse:

> **When you get divorced from a place where you've worked for five years, you realize you have to crank up old customers. It takes a real emotional toll.**

Paul Upham found that after his first assignment as an interim executive, he, too, had to crank up his network all over again:

121

> I focused all of my energies on the assignment, which *was* the right thing to do, but when I came back, I found my network in the East had dried up. It took thirty to sixty days of calling people to restart my network. The response I got from them was, "We thought you were fat, dumb, and happy out in Chicago and we took you off our radar screen."

If you're out of sight, you're out of mind. Therefore, the frequency of contact is almost as critical to successful networking as the quality of those contacts.

Seeking Specific Results

While the portable executive certainly approaches a network seeking results, this does not mean that every interaction must—or should—lead to specific results. Results come from relationships—good relationships—and thus relationship building naturally accounts for much of the non-results-oriented time one spends with other network members. As we will see later in this chapter, while the portable executive will indeed use his or her network to generate business, there is a subtle but clear difference in how this comes about in the context of a peer-peer network exchange. Over time, actual benefits evolve naturally from a well-developed network system where individuals truly get to know each other's core skills and attributes.

It is extremely important for the portable executive to continually broaden his or her network in order to get a more global view of what's happening both in the economy and in the community at large. Broadening your network increases your exposure to opportunity, which means extending your networks beyond business. When a portable executive engages in volunteer work, for example, the contacts he or she makes can serve as a basis for recommendations, particularly when the nature of the volunteer work involved exposes peers to talents or core skills not ordinarily tapped in one's business life. When Hans Solmssen made a career switch from the Lincoln Savings Bank in New York City to Magnetic Resonance Corporation, he had already served on the board of a private school with two of the company's investors. Says Solmssen:

> Two of the investors at Magnetic Resonance Corporation knew me well. I had been the chairman of the board of trustees of a small private school and they had sat on the board with me, so they knew how I reacted in tight, difficult situations and they knew I was unusually persistent and tenacious. They also knew me from our years together at the National Bank of Canada and saw me create a sizable, profitable bank from scratch.

Just How Informal Is Informal?

While networking is conducted on an informal basis, it is nevertheless a process that requires hard work and constant reassessment. Networking involves maintaining a delicate balance between meeting with people of different interests and core capabilities and ensuring that you're not wasting your time on activities that do not advance your purpose for being part of the network. Portable executive Ann Rarich recalls a time when "I was picking the wrong professional groups. They were comprised of people who weren't very genuine or sincere, and once I started to pick up on that, I found the group very unsatisfying. I needed to find the right network where I could really help and be helped."

Assessing the Value of the Network

To assess the true value of any given network, the portable executive must first commit to it long enough to be in a position to judge its function in helping her career. She must also work hard at her relationship within the network in order to reap whatever benefits the network can yield.

Portable executives are dependent upon network relationships for the success of their businesses. Not only are networks critical to the success of one's career, but the network is a portable executive's immediate business community and with it comes all of the attendant risks and rewards. There are two critical differences, however, between corporate culture and the network: All members of a network are viewed as valued peers. And the network constitutes an entirely flexible business community that can be adjusted according to need.

Types of Networks

All networks encompass various activities and offer a wide variety of value, but there are specific types of networks that the portable executive needs to be a part of in order to develop competitively.

LEARNING NETWORKS

I think it's important to talk and listen to people who have been networking for a while. Listen to their war stories. I think it will help your self-confidence to really get out there.

—Joseph Bevan

A commitment to continually learn is necessary for an executive to maintain and enhance the value of his core skills in the marketplace. As a portable executive moves toward self-direction, he needs to develop a substantial system to support this commitment to constant learning, and the network is a very important part of that. Through seminars and learning networks, the portable executive can find not only formalized training but also informal get-togethers where peers with complementary skills exchange current information and knowledge.

While verbal exchanges of information are a major function of networking, the portable executive must also mine all available resources in periodicals, books, computer networks, and databases in order to piece together and evaluate the information he needs. Information or intelligence gathering is an important facet of networking and encompasses a broad spectrum of activities, from participating in computer roundtable discussions, to knowing where and how to locate the most timely and most accurate information. Relationship building comes into play when the portable executive attempts to build relationships with either the authors of such periodical articles or the experts quoted in them. People identified and quoted in business and other periodicals are often flattered to be contacted and receptive to sharing further or more detailed information.

It should also be noted that the press can play a big part in networking efforts, as people who give quotes and information to the press do so not only to be noticed, but also to elicit a response from their audiences and gain feedback. Working through and with the press involves not only information gathering, but message sending, too.

NICHE NETWORKING GROUPS

Networks closely aligned with a particular business or issue provide a wealth of portable executives with whom you can form strategic alliances or partnerships. Often this type of network group allows a portable executive to call on others to supplement or support him on an assignment. Therefore, once you develop relationships within one niche group, you will have a pretty clear idea of which people within the network you can call on and trust to support you on a particular assignment. Jim Schwarz, an independent sales management consultant, described his own experience setting up this type of informal strategic alliance:

> When I was starting my own company, two people asked
> me to join their small organizations, which were already
> established. I decided not to because I really wanted my
> autonomy. But I suggested that we work on an alliance
> basis together—each of us does slightly different
> things—so when they need me, they bring me in, and
> when I need them, I bring them in.

Alliances such as this can be formed and disbanded on a pro-
ject-by-project basis or eventually evolve into actual partnerships
where groups from within a network begin to work together on a
regular basis.

THE SALES NETWORK

The sales network is undoubtedly the most results-oriented
type of network, as each network member is specifically seeking
to make sales. Quite simply, it is a tried-and-true network in
which satisfied clients recommend your services to someone else.
This type of network is certainly important, but the most important thing to remember about being part of a sales network is that
they build over time and are based solely on high-quality performance developed in the other types of networks listed previously.

Expanding the Network

Richard Achilles, a human resources executive who took early
retirement from IBM and today runs his own human resources
consulting firm, addressed one of the most important aspects of
maintaining one's network. Says Achilles:

> My network is strong and if you were to list everyone in
> the network, it would appear very extensive. But when
> you look at the realistic prospects for any one of the con-

tacts coming through with a work assignment in the short term, it would be very low—perhaps as low as only two or three percent. If you objectively assess your network, you will frequently recognize the need to expand your networking efforts further.

Essentially, the broader your network, the better your chances will be. But to make the most effective use of a network, you must be interested in it and contribute to it. Increasing the size and scope of your network enhances your ability to do both.

Networking for Support

First, you go around and share what happened to you when you were downsized. The next go-around, you say, "This is what I'm doing and now I'm looking for opportunities."

—Bob Hall

Throughout a portable executive's searching period, and particularly during the early periods of anxiety, networks can offer substantial practical and emotional support. Numerous formal support networks are available through outplacement programs and community groups. These groups, dedicated to executives in transition, are invaluable to newly downsized executives trying to adjust to their new roles. Eck Vollmer, a portable executive and former CFO of Gestetner, sought a mix of support within one network:

I'm a part of several groups. One is the Financial Executive Institute, or FEI, which offers support groups for unemployed executives. Within FEI, there are a number

127

of subgroups where I can find anything—support, placement, counseling, camaraderie—anything.

Ann Rarich found that getting involved with a nationwide international training house helped to ease the loneliness she felt
when she started her own business:

We were able to share professional practices and that
kind of thing, which was important because at that particular time there wasn't much in the way of a flexible
workforce or a tolerance for part-time workers. It helped
me to carve out my practice.

Places to Network

Networking may appear to be very informal, but developing a
good reliable network requires a lot of hard work. You cannot simply show up at a network gathering or industry conference hoping
to meet someone; you need to devote considerable thought to
what you are looking for and how you are going to obtain it. Following are several types of people who comprise networks, and
several different settings in which you will find them.

PERSONAL FRIENDS

Personal friends may not be the best business network, but
they do provide valuable support and a place to start. While many
of us have friends who are looking for jobs, we very often find we
can't help them. But personal friends are exactly that, and no executive should make the mistake of expecting his or her personal
friendships to fulfill their business networking purposes. The
portable executive is wiser to rely on his or her personal friends
primarily as a support network.

BUSINESS CONTACTS

The best place to begin your networking process is with your business contacts. These are the people who know you from a business setting and who probably have some understanding of who you are and what you have to offer a potential employer. (Remember, networking is a numbers game, and the more business contacts you have and can talk to, the better your chances of success.) Even if they themselves do not need your services immediately, very often they will know someone who does.

Bear in mind that your business contacts may not be strongly committed to supporting you, so don't get discouraged if they do not immediately come up with concrete ideas, particularly during the early stages of becoming portable, when you might be especially sensitive to a lukewarm response. Maintaining your business network—that is, letting them know where you are and what you're doing—is important in generating other networking opportunities. Be sure to capitalize on your personal business contacts, particularly in the early stages of building your network. They are stepping-stones to a broader, stronger network of referrals to other sources.

TRADE ASSOCIATIONS

One of the most formal network groups is the trade association, which offers a rapid introduction to a particular industry, thus affording portable executives a tremendous opportunity to learn while they are seeking to create a job. The biggest risk in joining a trade association to network is that you need to be careful not to spend all of your time with your competition. You must distinguish between associations that are, in effect, comprised of one's peers and those that contain potential customers or clients. In addition, trade associations often prove to be excellent sources of other professionals with whom one can form beneficial strategic alliances.

CONTINUING EDUCATION CENTERS

Colleges, universities, and continuing education centers that provide ongoing executive training offer a wealth of networking opportunities. As more and more universities focus on the mature market of continuing education, it is becoming easier to find and obtain catalogs and other sources of information that might aid an individual in his or her job creation. Continuing education centers also offer portable executives opportunities to participate on speaker's panels, give speeches, and teach, which, while appearing to be one-way activities, often result in potential clients or valuable networking contacts.

CHURCH AND/OR COMMUNITY SUPPORT GROUPS

Many local church and community support groups have sprung up around the country in response to the massive downsizings in the United States. These groups are specifically helpful in offering tremendous emotional support to those in the early stages of job creation. Relationships built during times of adversity often grow stronger over time and have the potential to evolve into beneficial alliances.

How to Approach Your Network

As the portable executive homes in on the type of business he or she wishes to create and begins to research the kinds of organizations that can aid in the process, they should also be making a list of the types of networks that seem to offer the greatest opportunities to learn and make business contacts.

Networking in its various types and forms may appear complex to the executive new to the portable mind-set, but it will soon become a way of life for the portable executive and will pervade all of his or her activities. As more executives join the ranks of the contingent workforce, we may well find networking at the top of the list of ways to communicate and develop business relationships and opportunities.

Networking today is very different than it was only a decade ago. As downsizings and restructurings continue to empty corporate office space, the business community is no longer conveniently located—and isolated—in the typical glass-and-steel buildings. The network is the business community for the 1990s and beyond.

Chapter Eight

ACTION PLANNING

◆

As the portable executive emerges from the searching period, he or she should have a good sense of the direction they want to take and the kind of business entities they want to create. The executive's self-assessment, information gathering, and experimentation, all of which transpired during the searching period, must now come together in an action plan that details the specific steps the executive will take to achieve success in creating their personal service business entities.

The portable executive approaches this planning phase having already undergone some critical attitudinal shifts during the searching period. Most important, she has come to appreciate her value as separate and distinct from the organization and, as a result, now has a vision of how she can employ her core skills in the marketplace. Through this process, the portable executive has, in effect, developed the mission portion of her action plan. By assessing her core skills and experimenting with possible applications of those skills, the portable executive has already envisioned what is possible in her future work lives. At this juncture, the portable executive also has a pretty clear sense of which employment vehicle is best suited for her, given her core skills and what she hopes to achieve. The employment vehicle that will enable an individual portable executive to carry out her action plan can range from operating as a sole practitioner on a contract basis, to acquiring an existing business to starting a new business or returning to a large organization as an employee.

Ongoing Planning

As the portable executive moves from the generalized transition phase to actual portability, it is important to realize that business planning is not a one-time activity, but a core process that the portable executive reviews, evaluates, and adjusts on an ongoing basis. Depending upon the individual's circumstances and requirements, this process can be as simple as planning a daily schedule, or as complex as comparing one's actual results with monthly benchmarks or creating a formal long-term action plan. The specific approach a portable executive takes will be influenced by both personal style and the employment vehicle she chooses, but it should be orderly and consistent since the action plan should serve her over time.

Organizational Planning Versus Self-planning

In assessing their attitudes, attributes, and core capabilities, portable executives come to understand themselves as personal service business entities rather than as employees of organizations. As you begin to develop your own action plan, recognize that as an independent business entity, you must weigh substantially different factors in your planning process than you did while employed by a large organization. For example, your action plan needs to account for the fact that as a portable executive you are limited by time, your individual mental and physical capabilities, and the availability of capital.

While many of the aspects of developing your action plan are taken from standard business planning procedures, there are essential differences as you are now involved in *self*-planning, not organizational planning. Following are the essential differences between the two:

133

ORGANIZATIONAL PLANNING VERSUS SELF-PLANNING

ORGANIZATION	PORTABLE EXECUTIVE
RESOURCES	
Expandable.	Limited.
AGENDA	
Controlled by the corporation.	Controlled by the individual.
BENCHMARKING	
Success measured by profitability.	Success measured by personal achievement.
TIME MANAGEMENT	
The life of an organization can be infinite.	The life of a human being is finite.
PRIORITIES	
Business forces.	Business, family, and community forces.

Although some self-planning should primarily encompass the nontraditional approach to creating a business that evolved during the searching period, traditional methods of creating a business plan should be considered as well. However, any solid business plan must incorporate a flexible series of steps or programs that can be adjusted to changes in the marketplace. The portable executive's self-plan must also anticipate the unavoidable changes that occur as life passes. The professional athlete's career, for instance, is an excellent example of the need to plan for changes that accompany aging.

Prior to discussing the nontraditional elements incorporated in a portable executive's planning, it is important to review the three traditional elements of a business plan that the portable executive must address: market research, competition, and financing.

134

Market Research

Throughout the searching phase of the job-creation process, you probably did a great deal of market research in order to come to an understanding of how best to employ your skills and capabilities in the marketplace. Analyzing marketplace realities is essential in creating any business plan, but it is particularly critical for you as a portable executive, since, as you will see in the next chapter, it significantly affects your action plan.

The more you know about the realities of the marketplace, the better able you will be to adapt and recombine your core capabilities. In the planning phase, your market research should *not* be broad-based, but rather aimed at defining applications, targeting markets, and identifying customer bases. Business owners Carol and Bob Frenier run a marketing business from their home in Vermont. Though the two spent many years producing commercials in Boston, today they work with dairy farmers placing ads on milk cartons.

The Freniers' initial market research helped them identify this untapped advertising potential. Then they discovered a unique niche for their business through more extensive market research. Says Carol Frenier:

> **We discovered that dairies have actual advertising media—which is the side of milk cartons. Radio and television stations are always looking for new media, and they also want to barter for it wherever they can because they are cash-poor. We bring the dairymen (who are basically nuts-and-bolts operation types of people) together with radio and TV stations where people sell air. We set up the barter. Since we administer it for the dairy, it is trouble-free for them. We've now taken it one step further: we are doing a three-way trade where we take the advertising space for the milk carton, sell it to a barter company that deals in media, which in turn pays us money, so we get our fee and pay the dairy for the carton.**

Carol and Bob Frenier's market niche development is an excellent example of how portable executives can use targeted market research to successfully tailor their offering to the realities of the marketplace. Since we as individuals are limited in physical and financial resources, the more targeted or niched your business is, the better off you'll be.

Competition

Every business entity contends with some form of competition. While the competitive source is not always clear to the individual executive, there is usually ample information to be gathered on one's competitors through networking, reading, and listening to potential and existing clients who have done some comparative shopping.

Since your competitive edge lies in your core capabilities and the ability to apply them effectively in the marketplace, an important part of creating a business plan involves developing an understanding of what the competition is doing, in order to distinguish your value from that of the competition's. It is not sufficient to simply know who your competitors are. You need to develop a sound sense of your competitors' strengths and weaknesses in order to sell into the market more effectively. Frequently, the best way to do this is to solicit feedback from clients about the service they are getting from the competition.

Often what gives you the edge in the marketplace is the very fact that you are portable. Marketing consultant Jim Schwarz, for instance, discovered that his competitive edge results from his ability to forge close relationships with his clients. They value his personal attention to detail, and certainly prefer it to the impersonal handling routinely offered by one of his larger competitors.

Finance

The portable executive must develop a traditional financial plan to project income, expense, cash flow, and capital requirements. While your business financial plan will intersect with your personal financial plan, they should be separate and distinct. The business financial plan will vary in complexity and detail depending on the type of employment vehicle you select. The most complex plans are those that involve starting a business or acquiring an existing business, while the least complex are those of the portable executive who elects to be employed by an organization again. A financial plan must be developed even by those who opt for traditional employment, as all executives need a financial plan to prepare for the changes that will occur in the course of their careers. Marketing executive Kathi Trepper, who began her career in the 1960s at Procter & Gamble, moved through several companies during her career before she was downsized out of TWA and ventured out on her own. Even before that, Trepper saw the necessity of creating a financial plan despite her full-time position:

> **The reality is that a company only hands you a paycheck for the days you're working, but it doesn't guarantee long-term. Not only are you expendable, but you don't have the opportunity to leave your mark on a company anymore. . . .**
>
> **Knowing this, I have an investment counselor and I read _Money_ magazine, the business section of the local paper, the _Wall Street Journal_, and the _New York Times_ business section on Sunday.**

Kathi Trepper's forward-looking financial planning is precisely what the portable executive needs. As Trepper said, in today's economy, you receive a paycheck only for the days you work.

The Reality of Portability

As a portable executive, you are on your own. You and you alone make the choices and decisions that will determine whether or not your plan is successful. This reality is substantially different from that of the organization employee engaged in business planning. Organizational planning, is, in effect, group planning. However, in some corporations where the CEO sets forth a plan, planning may not even be a group effort, but more dictatorial in nature.

Good planning requires a convergence of ideas, and accepting responsibility for your choices ultimately allows you to weigh each facet of your action plan and determine its influence on the outcome. Basically, it is your responsibility to balance the seemingly competitive traditional and nontraditional elements that comprise successful portability.

Continuity

Since lifetime employment no longer exists in the marketplace, as a portable executive you must concentrate on developing continuity of assignments that will yield a stable career path.

When compared to an organizational employee whose work is often defined as going to an office and maintaining a set routine, the type and flow of work for the portable executive can be pretty sporadic. As Dusty Bricker sees it:

> **Until I build a reputation for staging world-class business events, I think I have to be flexible and consider other methods of bringing in revenue.**

Planning the Expansion of Your Skill Base

In our knowledge-based society, the only way to add value in the marketplace is with an up-to-date, relevant set of core skills. Since your core skills and capabilities are your only real assets, it is essential to plan for their growth and expansion. Within the context of your business plan, you must account for the amount

138

of time you spend learning or preparing for future work against the amount of time you actually spend working.

When it comes to core skills, portable executives must plan:

1. How to objectively price their skills.
2. How to protect or insure their skills.
3. How to enhance or add value to them.
4. How to market them.

Limited Resources

One of the major factors that portable executives must adjust to and plan for is that, as individuals, they have only a certain capacity. One of the most common complaints heard from portable executives working alone is, "When you market, you can't work, and when you work, you can't market." While this serves to illustrate that an individual portable executive can do only so much alone, this and other problems can, as suggested earlier, often be overcome through the formation of strategic alliances, partnerships, or buying the services needed to augment business. During the start-up phase of his market research firm, John Trost came to understand it when:

> **I was staying up until 2:30 A.M. every night because I was handling production, staffing, and all of that stuff. One night, I realized what staff support was all about—we were truly overloaded with work and it occurred to me all of a sudden that this was not a very good way for me to spend my time.**

Financial Limitations

Financial limitations are closely related to the capability resource limitations mentioned above, and often extend beyond the simple economics of raising capital or generating income for a business. Since portable executives tend to seek an integrated, balanced lifestyle, the financial limitations that should be addressed in a business plan should include not only those issues directly related to running the business, but also personal cash-flow needs, such as the cost of the children's education, home maintenance costs, retirement savings, and any other major financial outlays that need to be projected over time. A business plan made by an executive in his early forties, working eighty-hour weeks, with three young children and a whopping mortgage, will obviously differ from that of an executive in his early sixties, who, though his children may be fully independent and the mortgage long since burned, nonetheless must adjust his plan for retirement needs, health-care contingencies, and the prospect of decreased work hours or full retirement. Since portable executives in many cases operate alone, they must also plan for business catastrophes that could affect their welfare as well.

Endgame Planning

One overriding reality that differentiates the situation of the portable executive from that of an employee of an organization is that it is usually assumed that the organization will exist indefinitely even though the players, personalities, and culture may change over time. This certainly makes business planning easier, as there is no need to plan for the "endgame." Portable executives, however, as individuals, are finite beings whose lives will one day end.

Elements of the Portable Executive's Plan

GUIDE TO ACTION

Once your direction has been fairly well established by the searching process, as a newly independent portable executive you may find yourself at a loss as you face the challenges and responsibility of planning your business. Since there is no one to approve or evaluate your plan other than yourself, it is less important that the plan look good on paper and far more important that it be a fully detailed, realistic document that will serve as a daily guide for action. This plan must function as an instrument of growth that will enable you to direct your limited resources to actions that will help you achieve your goals, both financially and personally. Financial consultant Dick West's action plan is simple, and he works with it on a regular basis:

> **It's not very neat. It's a yellow pad organized by major service categories, business evaluations, capital formation, mergers and acquisitions, and I try to work a portion of each day in each of those service categories.**

TIME MANAGEMENT

As a portable executive, your greatest asset—second only to your core skills—is your time. Therefore, the time-management aspects of business planning are critical to your effectiveness. Organizing the data within your plan and estimating completion dates for projects prove extremely useful in helping you focus on those activities that are beneficial to your business. Initially, this process will be based on guesstimates and gut feelings, but over time you will develop a sound sense of what can and what cannot be accomplished during a given time period. For those who wish to manage their time on their computers, there are several time-management software packages available for this purpose, such as Lotus Organizer, Sharkware, or Timeslips, to name a few. For others, a daily "To Do" list serves just as well. Advertising executive Bud Titsworth, for example, routinely sets aside an hour a day to plan the marketing for his business. When activities such as this are planned in advance, it enables you to keep all aspects of running your business intact.

BENCHMARKING

In large organizations, performance is periodically measured and reviewed against the goals set by the company for the individual executive. The process of benchmarking performance is equally important for you as a portable executive, as your measure of success must reside within yourself and should not be derived from outside institutions. Incorporating benchmarks into your plan provides a disciplined way of objectively measuring your achievement against your goals. Portable executive Sam Marks, who has undertaken over thirty "temporary executive" assignments, keeps a diary of his activities with clients:

> **The diary is an invaluable tool. I call it my reality diary. The most important part of it is that I have my tasks written down in it, so I can review my activities and give myself a report card. I ask, "What behavior did I change today?" and I establish a benchmark of where we started. Then I ask, "Am I making change? Is the firm making headway?" It's a report card for both me and the client. It tells me if I've developed my milestones correctly. It shows me if I'm navigating correctly, or if I'm ten degrees off or twenty degrees off.**

As Sam Marks's comments suggest, for him, the diary is a highly individualized and precise check-and-balance system. While the diary system may not appeal to you, every portable executive must address the challenge of creating a disciplined benchmarking system of his own.

RANKING PRIORITIES

You will quickly recognize that in viewing yourself as an independent business entity, no aspect of your life can be excluded from the planning process. As you plan your schedule, it will become clear that allocating time for family, community, and other nonwork-related activities must be balanced in your overall planning if you are going to achieve your personal and professional goals. This process offers you the positive benefit of integrating all of the aspects of your life and adopting a more holistic lifestyle.

Types of Plans

The type of plan that you develop as a portable executive is usually colored by your personality, and is often influenced by what you would like to see happen, rather than by what is reasonable to expect. If you have ever been part of a planning process within a large organization, you will recognize the basic types of plans that consistently emerge. The following examples are meant to serve as guidelines in helping you to formulate your own plan. As you review them, you will see the potential traps inherent in the planning process and be able to evaluate your own thinking in light of these examples. Keep in mind as you read them that the best plan for you will most likely involve combining a number of different aspects found in each of these plans.

THE PLACID WATER PLAN

The assumption behind this plan is that things will remain pretty much the same as they have always been. As such, the Placid Water Plan is simply a plan that serves as a building block for the future. It relies heavily on past trends, which, while offering a good, safe place to start, often do not account for the changes in the global marketplace. This plan demands that you take a good hard look at the past, learn from it, and accept what is valid in that assessment, but it fails to incorporate significant current marketplace changes that are crucial to your ultimate success.

THE SKI SLOPE PLAN

The Ski Slope Plan represents the ultimate optimistic view of continued success and exponential growth ad infinitum. Portable executives on the whole, and particularly those just starting out, are often tremendously excited by their offering and are therefore vulnerable to falling into this trap. The person who creates this type of plan probably has not done enough market research or competitive analysis to inject sufficient information about the realities of the marketplace into his planning. No company, no matter how well planned, can grow on a straight-upward trajectory forever. Adjustments to a plan such as this must account for those independent variables, such as limited time, limited energy, and other nonwork-related priorities.

THE HOCKEY STICK PLAN

The Hockey Stick Plan incorporates the reality that during the start-up stages of a business there are likely to be struggles, difficult challenges, and flat, or even negative, performance periods before the business takes off. After the initial struggle, one's business can catch on and produce the same upward trajectory of growth as seen in the Ski Slope Plan. This plan prepares you realistically for a slow period in the beginning, but it is important to time your "takeoff" correctly, or else it is possible this plan will not be achieved.

THE SWISS ALPS PLAN

The Swiss Alps Plan illustrates the peaks and valleys many experience in developing a new business. This view is, in fact, closer to everyday reality than the others but cannot accurately predict when, realistically, the peaks and valleys in the marketplace will occur.

TWO STEPS FORWARD, ONE STEP BACK

The plan called Two Steps Forward, One Step Back is the most realistic—it is optimistic enough to reflect a general pattern of growth but also acknowledges that there will be ups and downs. It also suggests that you step back to assess and evaluate every period of growth to make sure that the growth is solid and to plan the next move upward. With this type of plan in place, you can quickly adjust to periods of growth and adversity, as it allows you to monitor and assess the progress being made *before* you commit your efforts and resources to the next project.

Pipe Dreams Versus Reality

One of the biggest challenges in the planning process is to be sure that you don't create a plan that is so optimistic that you will never achieve it or so pessimistic that you don't really grow, or achieve your goals. There is no better feeling in the world than to actually realize your dream, and if you plan realistically, its achievement becomes possible.

In coming to view yourself as a business entity, you eventually begin to think like an owner and CEO. You realize almost simultaneously that while you are responsible for the whole show, you can't possibly do everything alone. You learn to deal with and, in some cases, expand upon your limited capacity. And you have the ultimate thrill of controlling and growing your business and achieving your goals.

There are many challenges for you to meet as a portable executive: devising marketing plans, setting up an office, and, most important of all, planning for the maintenance and growth of your portable skills. These exciting facets of portability will be addressed in the next chapter and in the balance of the book.

Chapter Nine

MAINTAINING YOUR
PORTABLE SKILLS

◆

There's an old saying that "gettin' there firstes' with the mostes' " is the key to a successful and rewarding career, and it's a motto every portable executive should live by. Later, in our chapter on marketing, we'll discuss how the portable executive can get there "first" but the focus of this chapter is on how to get there with the "most," which for the portable executive means getting there with world-class portable skills.

As we have seen, the knowledge-based economy we live in has created a demand for executives who maintain their skills at the highest level of proficiency. Technological advances have handed us an information universe of staggering proportions, and one in which anyone who can operate a personal computer has access to that knowledge. Consequently, portable executives need to understand not only that their skills are their most valuable asset, but, more important, they must figure out how to continually maintain and enhance their skill bases within the ever-expanding knowledge universe. Each individual executive must also discern which skills to develop, and which skills, when subjected to a straight cost-benefit analysis, are best subcontracted out to others. (By "cost-benefit analysis," we mean simply that the portable executive needs to allot money and time for the development of their core skills and skills that will create new income streams, but must not waste time or financial resources developing skills that do not enhance their core competencies or which take time away from productively employing their core skills.) Cost systems advisor Jack Cahill, for example, finds that the simplest and most cost-effective method of deciding which of his skills to develop at any given time is to ask someone in his network of potential clients what their critical needs are.

Attitude Toward Skills

Since their core skills are both their greatest asset and their entire inventory, portable executives must learn that developing and maintaining them is *not* an optional investment. All too often—and particularly when financial resources are limited—executives make the mistake of viewing skill development and maintenance as secondary to servicing clients. But it is critical for you as a portable executive to view skill maintenance and development as an investment in the quality of your business, and to allot sufficient resources for it. Otherwise, you're apt to find another portable executive with up-to-date skills snatching your market share.

You will occasionally have to invest both time and money in skill development, which will take you away from client service. But it's a short-term trade-off, as you may be giving up income right now in favor of the benefits to be derived from improving your skill base and your ability to generate fees in the long run.

Jim Schwarz, a former senior vice president of training and development for a consulting firm, commented on the proportion of time he spent there on skill development compared to the time he now allots to it as a portable executive:

> **While at the consulting firm, I went to one class. Since I've been on my own, I have probably spent ten times more time on my own training than the firm ever did,**

particularly in strategy implementation and managing organizational change. I have refined myself and become an expert in areas I once didn't even know about.

Committing to an ongoing plan for increasing and broadening one's knowledge and skill base, as Jim Schwarz has, is what sets the portable executive apart from the pack.

Each individual must also seriously consider which skills are worth developing and which are more cost-effective to acquire. Some skills are more valuable than others, and while value is relative to the individual, it is important to make solid, cost-effective decisions about which skills to invest in. In a knowledge-based society, the greatest threat to the portable executive is personal obsolescence. It is therefore imperative that executives choose the most appropriate skills to maintain and develop.

Generalists Are Specialists

There is a simple answer to the age-old discussion about whether we need more generalists or more specialists in management: The answer is that we need *both*. In today's economy, however, the person who is a generalist must specialize in performing as a generalist. Pitney Bowes's Vice President Northeast Division, Ernest M. (Chuck) Jackson, Jr., describes how an executive possessing generalist skills as a manager can remain flexible:

No one can specialize in everything, and frankly I think you don't have to. If you say to yourself, "These are the items I need to help me make a decision," and then you gather the essential data, you are becoming "portable." If you are flexible enough to listen for information and understand it, you're not only a good manager, you can go almost anywhere.

Holmes Bailey, a portable executive who works on financial turnarounds, describes his core skills:

> My attitude is that it doesn't make any difference what the business is—good management skills are needed universally. When I went to MIT's Sloan School of Management, nobody said "We're training you for the aviation industry," or "We're training you for the vacuum industry." Nobody said that. Core skills are [just] the skills you need to be successful in America in business.

Indeed, Bailey's track record supports his supposition that he can apply his skills in any business. As he describes a typical assignment, however, it becomes clear that he is more than just a specialist in financial reengineering:

> You take a company that's unprofitable and shrinking. You put in the time, energy, and talent it takes to make it profitable, then staff it with people who can help it grow and run it into the future. The key is to find people you can hire . . . people you can train who will keep the business going and growing for the next twenty years.

Bailey focuses on completely renewing the companies that engage him, and what he accomplishes ranges far beyond simply turning them around financially. He redevelops these companies to make them viable over the long term. To that extent, his skill base supports not only his role as a specialist in financial turnarounds but as a generalist as well. Just as the portable executive who focuses on a highly defined market niche succeeds by building a reputation within a particular segment of the market, so too can executives who specialize in being generalists develop substantial reputations.

Developing a reputation for delivering a particular expertise and consistently maintaining that expertise is critical to the portable executive's success. Professional service firms have often said that the major source of new business is satisfied clients. This also rings true for the portable executive as he or she gains a reputation as an expert in a particular field.

Applicability of Skills

As your skills evolve, it quickly becomes apparent that the depth of knowledge and understanding of a particular subject or area of business is less important than how you apply that knowledge throughout the lifetime of your career. The successful portable executive understands the need for continuous learning as well as the ability to translate that learning into real-time delivery of services to clients and employers. In the old hierarchical system of organizations, very little premium was placed on new ideas or new applications, but in the new knowledge-based system, the ability to apply knowledge is one of the key ingredients of job continuity and career security. When one understands how critical the ability to apply knowledge in today's marketplace truly is, it follows that the portable executive has to develop an intensely focused expertise in order to achieve real value.

Skill-Set Analysis

In order to most effectively use their skill sets, portable executives must possess a clear understanding of which skills they already have and which skills they still need to acquire. The exercises in chapter five, aimed at identifying both one's core capabilities and attributes, no doubt exposed some major gaps in every executive's repertoire. How the individual addresses these deficiencies and begins to upgrade his or her existing skills is key to the portable executive's success.

A simple way to evaluate your skill inventory is to categorize your skills into three distinct sets, enabling you to prioritize them and decide how to maintain and acquire new skills on an ongoing basis.

Core Skills

Every individual who has reached management or executive level in their career has attained a certain degree of expertise with a set of core skills he can rely upon. It is critical that the portable executive understand the value of his core skills both to himself and in the marketplace.

A quick study of the typical career path of an individual who has worked in an organization reveals a common pattern. The first ten years are usually devoted to the acquisition of core skills, while the next ten to fifteen are dedicated to learning how to apply these skills. The remainder of an executive's career is spent using the wisdom gleaned from his experience to effect positive change for the organization he works for.

Dick Swank, a former executive vice president of Dun & Bradstreet, initially decided during his searching period that he did not want to work full-time in another organization. When he was asked to consider a consulting position, he recalls telling the principals:

> **I'm uniquely qualified to do this job for you because one of the things I was responsible for at Dun & Bradstreet was technical publishing, and the technical publishing subsidiary is roughly the same size, the same basic business. All of my skills apply.**

As negotiations progressed, the offer on the table was switched from consultant to a full-time position as Edgell Communications' chief executive officer. Says Swank:

151

> I'd really made a promise to myself when I left Dun &
> Bradstreet that I was not going to go back into a situa-
> tion where I'd be working eighty to ninety hours a week.
> So I said no.

Even though he rejected the offer, Swank did agree to go home
and think about it. When he told his wife Jean about it, he said,
"If ever there were a job that was cut out just for me, this job is it,
because I know exactly what to do." Soon, he was waking up in
the middle of the night thinking about it. Despite the fact that
he'd decided not to return to a full-time position—let alone one
that would require working ninety-hour weeks and commuting to
Cleveland from his home in Connecticut—Edgell Communications had found their new CEO.

Dick Swank knew his skill set, offered years of expertise, and
had developed a driving passion for applying his skills over the
course of his career. His was truly a situation where the core skills
he'd developed over a lifetime proved to be so perfectly matched
to the assignment that he could not turn his back on the challenge.

Transferability

All portable executives need to develop the ability to *apply*
their core skills in a multitude of ways that offer real value in the
marketplace. It is important to recognize that this ability goes far
beyond the question of marketing. An executive with a core expertise in selling consumer products, for example, can transfer
that expertise to selling services within a very short period of
time. He simply needs to shift from the specifics of selling a hard
product to the relational selling required in a service business.
Allen Grossman is a prime example of someone who employed
his core skills to manage two vastly different types of businesses
successfully—moving from a regional paper and packaging distribution company to become the CEO of Outward Bound. These

quantum skill-application shifts are achieved only when the portable executive engages in an intensive assessment of his or her core skills and attributes and then develops both to the point that a career shift can naturally evolve.

Natural Skills

Natural skills are skills that an individual already possesses that can easily be developed into core skills. Natural skills are the skills that career changes are made of, since they offer the portable executive both the greatest challenge and the most opportunity. And because these are innate skills, they can be developed very rapidly. When Joe Cullen took an interim position putting together a national distribution warehouse for the United Auto Workers, one of his assignments was to train one of his own employees and his supervisor. Cullen, who had never been involved in training before, soon discovered a natural talent for teaching that gave him an all-time high. Keith Darcy, who had moved successfully up the corporate ladder as a banker in his early career, realized that his natural skills and interests concerned ethics and values in the marketplace. This realization eventually led to the development of his own foundation dedicated to the study of ethics in leadership.

It is often tricky for the emerging portable executive to determine how to apply her natural skills and to what degree she should commit to developing them. Of course, this requires a commitment of time and capital which, when used to further natural skills, takes away from further development of existing core skills. The answer to this question can only be found in discovering how deeply one feels about using one's natural skills. For many, the depth of passion that arises at the prospect of aligning their work lives with their natural skills is the deciding factor, while for others, searching for creative ways to apply their natural skills in a way that is personally satisfying in an existing position may be the appropriate balance. Clearly, the portable executive who can combine both her natural and core skills will have the best of both worlds. Eileen O'Kane, for instance, used her natural talent for art to become a chef, which eventually lead to her becoming a restaurant entrepreneur.

Developing a Natural Skill into a Core Skill

The development of one's natural skills is often rapid due to the individual's inborn talent. The portable executive does, however, need to decide how much time and effort he is willing to invest in trying to develop a natural skill into a core skill. Both Manny Elkind, who found a way to pursue his vocation and switch his career path while still employed by Polaroid, and Keith Darcy, who left banking to pursue his passion for ethics, undertook a great deal of work in transforming their natural skills into core skills. Both strengthened their knowledge base by taking courses and reading in those areas unfamiliar to them, putting all of their energy behind their dreams of developing their natural skills into businesses. The key here is learning how to gauge how steep your learning curve will be during a transition of this magnitude and planning accordingly. Attention must be paid to whether one's natural skills will be worthwhile in the marketplace once developed, as the economics of skill development and maintenance are a serious consideration in establishing a plan for business creation.

Generalist Skills

Generalist skills are basically skills that anyone can acquire and which, in most cases, are more economical (both from a financial and a time-management point of view) to purchase. Accounting, basic business law, insurance, and marketing are all examples of generalist skills. Whether the portable executive chooses to develop any of them is strictly up to the individual, but remember it is wise to subject these skills to a simple cost-benefit analysis before making a decision. In writing a business book for high school students, Frank Gilabert decided to buy the printing, marketing, and distribution expertise from professionals in each of those fields so that he could publish the book by himself. In doing so, he retained a focus on quality control for his book, and was able to spend his time writing and doing research.

Regardless of whether the portable executive chooses to buy generalist skills or develop his or her own, these are important skills to which every emerging portable executive must pay close attention. This is particularly true for those establishing their own businesses or acquiring existing businesses. But the decisions one makes about developing or acquiring certain generalist skills will often change over time, as one's skills change and the marketplace changes. A sole practitioner in marketing, for example, may choose to produce his or her own direct-mail campaign with the aid of a desktop publishing package, handle accounting needs with the addition of some accounting software, and handle the legal and insurance needs while the business remains small. As business grows, however, these generalist skills should be passed off to others as quickly as possible in order to maximize the time the portable executive spends applying core skills in the marketplace.

Computer Literacy

While some executives group computer literacy with generalist skills, the portable executive truly cannot afford not to be computer literate. For those portable executives who work alone, computer literacy must be developed to the level of a core skill. If you are not computer literate—even if you subcontract out all of your word processing, accounting, and marketing—you are closing yourself off from the constantly expanding knowledge universe. The research capabilities, networking opportunities, databases, and other knowledge readily available to computer users cannot be ignored by any portable executive who expects to thrive.

How to Maintain Your Skills

Consider the professional athlete. There is no better model of skill maintenance and no better illustration of how concentration, continuous practice, and coaching can raise one's level of performance.

Like the professional athlete who benefits from a coach or trainer's suggestions and objective assessment of his or her performance, you, too, could adopt a series of coaches or trainers in your quest for continuous learning. Some peer groups engage in cross-coaching of this nature and have actually formalized the process by hiring accountants, lawyers, and other consultants to coach members of the group.

One of the critical reasons for practicing and upgrading one's portable skills is the continual explosion of knowledge in today's marketplace. You just can't let your skill maintenance slip for any period of time or, like a professional athlete who is laid off due to injury, it'll take twice as much effort to get back to the same level of performance.

On-the-Job Training

Just as most executives spend the first ten or fifteen years of their careers developing and learning to apply their core skills within organizations, the portable executive will receive much of his or her skill maintenance and development on the job. In a business setting, it becomes easier for the portable executive to identify ways of applying his or her skills and to receive the feedback necessary to improve performance. However, while feedback and objective performance appraisal may have been supplied by the organizations the portable executive once worked for, part of becoming portable involves developing methods of measuring success that are independent of an organization.

The standards of measurement within any given company are specific to that company's purposes and do not offer full-time employees or sole practitioners with a portable-executive mentality an objective means of measuring their growth and capability development in the marketplace. Portable executives must take the initiative to obtain feedback from their clients in order to enhance the value of their on-the-job learning.

Portable executives should also consider whether a job or assignment they are offered provides them with any means of skill maintenance or development. Marketing consultant John Trost says: "I'm working for firms that are basically on the edge. It's on-the-job training to work with those kinds of people because I'm pushed to my limits." If a given job does not offer a substantial means of growth, an executive should probably not spend a lot of time in it. At the very least, the portable executive who takes an assignment or job with a flat growth expectation should identify and create the opportunity to learn within it. Portable executive Dusty Bricker says:

> I guess I am the type of person who looks at a multiple-choice question and wants an answer that's not among the choices. When I was in a corporation, I wanted to create things that didn't exist. So if I quickly identify what I'm supposed to do, then I can begin wondering how things could be done a bit differently.

Giving Talks, Speeches, and Serving on Panels

Giving talks, speeches, and serving on panels, although primarily marketing tools, are actually two-way learning streets. The process of preparing for these activities alone presents the portable executive with a way to enhance his or her skills, and audience feedback often serves to refine and develop the material with each successive presentation. Over the past ten years, there has been a tremendous explosion of trade publications and seminars (which focus on various niche audiences) that provide excellent learning and marketing opportunities. Niche publications generally need material, and portable executives will find the trade media open to receiving articles. Once you have published an article or two, it becomes easier to obtain speaking engagements or positions on panels.

Buying Skills

One way the portable executive can acquire skills is to hire a professional and learn as much as possible from the person providing you with a service. For example, if you hire an accountant or a lawyer during the start-up phase of your business, you can then use this basic knowledge to handle those activities yourself.

Though cost should be considered, there are instances when buying skills in this way serves also as a means of improving your own skill base and should be considered part of the investment process. Marketing specialist Carol Frenier hired an accountant for the first six months that she was in business and then took it from there:

> I hired an accountant who did a great job, helping me to do projection spreadsheets. I've got a regular bookkeeping system and a good custom-made spreadsheet that does cash flow and accruals, which let me look a year or two out. I do all my own financial stuff in-house, but I send the finished products to the bookkeeper to review them for me.

Formal Education

Just as many professions require that an individual take a certain number of continuing-education credits each year, the portable executive needs to develop his own course of continuing education based on the core skills they have chosen to employ. Trade and professional associations, local universities, and various adult education programs all offer opportunities for upgrading one's skills. In addition, the portable executive needs to stay on top of all current developments within his field through reading professional journals, and attending industry-oriented peer group discussions or round tables.

As the portable executive weighs the means he will use to improve, develop, and maintain his skills, some further thoughts on skill development are worth mentioning. In a world in which the doubling rate of knowledge seems to be outstripping everyone's ability to keep up, the portable executive can easily become overwhelmed by the prospect of what it will take to maintain and develop a marketable skill base. The most important thing to remember is that while the world as a whole is changing rapidly, the basic underlying knowledge in any given area of expertise develops far more slowly. It is therefore the ability to apply knowledge that counts. As Joe Cullen pointed out in an earlier chapter, when his colleagues possessed only a smattering of knowledge on a subject, the reading he did in a few trips to the library made him an "instant expert" and enabled him to apply his core skills in a new way.

It is not as important to be *the* leading expert in a given area of knowledge or business as it is to know how to apply your core skills. Then, as you assess the skills you will need to complete any given project, and gauge how long it will take to obtain or develop additional skills, you need only look to the ever-growing circle of portable executives to realize that someone with just the right skills to augment and complement your own is probably just a phone call away.

Chapter Ten

MARKETING
AND SALES

◆

No matter how successful an executive has been while working within a large organization, in the world of portability, it is never enough to possess top-flight skills. The portable executive's career is equally dependent upon his or her ability to communicate those skills to potential and existing clients.

In the early seventies, when the ban on advertising and solicitation of accounting services was lifted, John Thompson's partners at KMG Main Hurdman wanted to run out and hire "salesmen." But John said, "That's not going to do any good, because people buy accounting from accountants. We're just going to have to learn how to do this ourselves." What ensued was a long period of coached study, during which the accountants at KMG Main Hurdman learned how to convey to their clients and potential clients both the value of their services and how those services could address their clients' specific needs. They became effective in marketing and selling their own services, which is precisely what each emerging portable executive must learn to do.

While much of what we discuss in this chapter may seem geared to the sole practitioner, remember that the basic common denominators—marketing and sales—apply to all portable executives, including those, like John and his former partners at KMG Main Hurdman, who choose to work within organizations.

One of the top priorities for all portable executives is to learn how to communicate the value and applicability of their skills in the marketplace. This challenge may at first seem daunting to the executive who has had little or no marketing or sales experience. For this reason, many a portable executive has been tempted, as John's partners were, to buy a sales force and leave the selling to them. Even if an executive does eventually employ a sales force, it is critical that he understand the essential challenges and unique elements of marketing and sales as they apply to the services he is offering.

The Marketing and Sales Funnel

The goal of any successful marketing and sales effort is to guide potential clients through a conversion process, which essentially involves five elements. The first is for the portable executive to make her offering known to those who are unaware of it. From there, one needs to supply information to those who express curiosity about one's offering. The third step in the process is to begin to educate those who express interest in the offering, and finally, in the fourth and fifth steps of marketing, the portable executive seeks to convert interested potential clients into first-time buyers and eventually into the group that represents the backbone of any business: repeat customers.

In most businesses, the line between marketing and sales is often blurred. Sole practitioners, in particular, may find themselves creating a marketing strategy, making all of the sales calls themselves *and* negotiating and closing their own sales. It is important, however, for the portable executive developing a business to understand the key distinctions between marketing and sales in order to develop a consistent strategy and appropriately allocate their resources. Recall the working definitions of marketing and sales:

161

- *Marketing*—The process of continuously informing both users and potential users about the nature and application of one's product or service. Success in marketing is measured by the number of leads developed.
- *Sales*—The function of sales is to negotiate an agreement with the client to buy one's product or service. Success in sales is measured by the number of deals one closes.

Since each of these activities has a different measure of success, it is important to understand the subtle shift that occurs both in the message the portable executive sends to the client and how the relationship one has with the client changes after a successful negotiation has been met.

The Four Basic Elements of Marketing

All marketing efforts can be distilled to four basic steps, and once the portable executive understands how each functions, it will help to clarify the confusion that may result as the complexity and nuances of marketing are introduced. In the simplest terms, the four basic elements of marketing are:

1. Defining the market for one's product or service.
2. Crafting and packaging the message.
3. Selecting the vehicle or media for one's message that will most effectively reach one's market.
4. Conveying the message consistently over time.

Defining the Market

I had to go through the discipline of actually defining what it was I was trying to sell and who I was trying to sell it to.

—Richard Achilles

All portable executives need to define the target market for their product or service. This process involves looking at people in the broad sense of potential customers and deciding which of them are most likely to purchase your product or service. This is called target market definition. Niche players, like Carol Frenier in her milk-carton/media-bartering business, and Frank Gilabert, who writes books for high school students, zero in on their target market as they define (and refine) their offerings. The majority of portable executives, however, must first identify their target market before they can begin developing their marketing plans.

As you begin to determine who your target market is, the size of your potential market can be quite daunting. Two key points help narrow it down. First, decide which potential customers you can communicate with, then estimate how many of them you can actually service if they do become customers.

You probably already have a sense of who your target market is, based upon your work during the searching process and business creation periods. For instance, portable executive Sam Marks, who specializes in marketing and strategic planning, decided during his searching period to focus on servicing professional service companies, while Anne Rarich, who specializes in training and development, decided to concentrate her efforts on companies that need help in management development. Focusing on a target market in this way helps ensure that your marketing materials are addressing likely buyers of your services.

Once you have identified your market, you'll need to research and identify specific targets to whom you will direct your message. Armed with this research, you can then use your network contacts to identify specific groups or individuals within companies who should be made aware of your offering. This is probably the most effective method of identifying, and connecting with, appropriate individuals in the target market.

Invariably, as a portable executive, you must determine whether you will derive greater benefits from conducting extensive market research or from making random "cold" calls on prospective clients. On the one hand, devoting considerable amounts of time to conducting market research may well yield a list of "perfect customers," which will enable you to tailor your message and concentrate your efforts on "selling" to that specific audience. On the other hand, if you decide not to spend as much time on targeting the market, you will be sending your message to a far broader universe and will, as a result, need to spend more time doing follow-up. No matter which strategy you employ, you must remember to allocate appropriate levels of money and time to reach the optimum number of potential customers.

In defining your market, you must consider a number of factors:

- Is the offering so specialized that the group of potential users is highly defined? Or is it so broad that identification is virtually impossible?
- Are you prepared to cope with the failure—or the *success*—of a broad-based marketing program? A company launching the sale of telephone horoscopes in Los Angeles expected an estimated 5,000 calls the first day. Instead, they got 30,000, and the demand increased from there.
- Know the purpose of each specific marketing activity and evaluate the response to it accordingly. For example, if you are trying to create awareness, don't measure results by the number of orders received.

Creating Your Message

There are four basic elements that the portable executive should include in his or her marketing message:

1. A clear understanding of the customers' needs.
2. A clear statement of how the service or product meets those needs.
3. A clear indication of how the offering is distinguishable from the competition.
4. Believability.

Most portable executives agree that putting together their message was one of the hardest things they had to do. Human resources executive Richard Achilles said:

> **Putting my thoughts together in a concise and penetrating way was very, very difficult. I was in my study most of every day and night for over a week. I had more arguments with myself during that one week than I have before or since. I studied the honesty and veracity of the statements I was making and the degree of service I could deliver. I didn't do it casually. The message was scrubbed down to "This is what I can do."**

Achilles's experience reflects some of the reasons why creating a marketing message is so difficult. Portable executives just starting out are not sure exactly how to present what they are offering in a way that is honest, accurate, and attractive to potential customers. Developing one's message involves a process of experimentation that evolves over time and is affected by the actual results the portable executive obtains. Therefore, even though creating the message is critically important, one should not spend a protracted amount of time agonizing over it. Develop brochures and other promotional materials as soon as possible, and go to press with an early version. These materials will evolve as one's business does, and the relatively low cost of production makes it affordable for the portable executive to produce new materials as the need arises.

The most important point of any message is that it is flexible enough to evolve, as one's business does, to reflect any changes, improvements, or new market focuses. Also, when creating a message, portable executives must be sure not to focus too much on their competency and skill set and not enough on the customer's needs. Messages that blatantly blow the presenter's horn are destined to turn off potential clients.

Content of the Message

The ideal is to come up with a tag line or headline that describes in broad terms what you're offering. Don't try to force it, however, as both will eventually emerge as one's business does. When the right headline or tag line does emerge, you'll recognize it, but remember to keep it simple, since most people don't read details unless the headline catches their eye. You may also choose to vary the tone of your head- and tag lines depending on the circumstances. IMCOR's running shirts, for example, feature the humorous message, "CEOs to GO," while the headline on their other promotional materials, "Contract Managers: A Flexible Management Option," is more serious in tone. Both are appropriate in their respective places.

While one's message should contain adequate text to inform the client, it should be stated simply and in straightforward terms designed to pique the reader's interest. Concrete examples and case studies that demonstrate the business's usefulness to the potential client helps him envision how his own needs might be served. It can also be very helpful to disclose the names of "satisfied clients" in one's marketing materials to present a credible track record. It is absolutely critical, however, to obtain permission to use these names, as many people tend to be sensitive about having their names appear in brochures and other types of literature.

One of the toughest problems an emerging portable executive faces is selling himself before he's gotten any assignments. This can be dealt with, however, through detailing previous work experiences in one's marketing materials or creating hypothetical case studies that are clearly labeled as such. Here, the portable executive can capitalize on his core capabilities and the proven strengths and attributes that he identified during the searching phase.

Create an Upbeat, Accurate Message

The message you send should be upbeat and positive. Your pride and enthusiasm for your offering should shine through without overstating your abilities or making promises that can't be delivered. One way to avoid sending a "puffed up" message is to step back and review each message to determine whether you can truly deliver the quality your message claims you can.

This touches on the last essential element of message creation: believability. The portable executive must recognize that since most people receiving the message are not initially receptive to it, anything that strikes them as incredible will surely make them more resistant to it. For example, if the industry standard turnaround time for delivering a bound report is twenty days and your message says you can do it in five, that in and of itself may make the audience doubt the credibility of your message and your product. It would be better to say "fast turnaround" and save the specifics until you have the opportunity to explain your approach in greater detail.

The Limits and Potential of Your Message

Attempting to craft a message that will convey a universal application of your offering to your target group is next to impossible. Very few marketing messages, such as Nike's "Just Do It," are superstars; most are merely adequate.

It takes a great deal of time to evolve the right message, and even then one must be willing to review and revise it as one's business matures and develops. A message must be informative in nature, designed to raise an awareness, pique one's interest, and will not necessarily "sell" the product or service. For this reason, after each new client experience, the portable executive should consider how that particular experience affects or changes the message. Try the message out on potential buyers and ask for their feedback. Creating a message is not a natural process for most people; it takes time and a great deal of patience to develop the right one.

Distinguishing Yourself from the Competition

As many of us have observed in viewing different TV commercials, mentioning the competition's name in an attempt to distinguish your product or service can easily backfire. The old saying in advertising that "no matter how your name is mentioned, having it mentioned at all is positive" is largely true. More important, though, is that the portable executive should spend less time focusing on the competition and more time focusing on the unique qualities of his or her own offering. The portable executive's service will ultimately be purchased on a repeat basis for its value to the client, not for its difference from the competition.

Vehicles for Conveying Your Message

The vehicle or vehicles portable executives choose to convey their marketing message will depend on a number of factors, including:

- The size of the marketing budget.
- The size of audience (mass market or target audience).
- The nature of the offering itself.

Below are discussions of some of the most effective vehicles.

Verbal Communication

A face-to-face meeting with a potential client is the most effective way to convey the nature of your offering. As executive Joseph Bevan put it:

To really make it happen, you have to commit more effort. You have to work harder and knock on more doors.

In-person meetings are clearly selling opportunities. Though they often require a great deal of time and expense, they offer the opportunity to tailor your offering to the clients' needs and the chance to further interest clients. The objective, of course, is to move the sale along, but it is often difficult to determine how far to go in the first meeting. If you sense that it is not the right time to attempt to close the transaction, set up another meeting, volunteer to supply further information, or offer to enter into a tryout situation with the client. A former vice president of marketing for Eveready Battery, Dave Thorpe, does a masterful job of helping potential customers share their professional problems, which makes it far easier for them to identify the ways in which he can help them. Face-to-face meetings should always heighten a potential client's awareness of your offering and deepen your understanding of the client's needs.

Letters or Correspondence

Personal letters offer an effective means of conveying your message to a highly defined target audience. Your correspondence should always be tailored to the particular client to whom you are writing, and be as personal as possible, and as succinct as possible.

According to the newsletter *Clips & Tips*, if you answer the following questions in your letter, you are more likely to make a sale:

1. What will you do for me if I listen to your story?
2. How are you going to do this?
3. Who is responsible for the promises you make?
4. Who else have you done this for?
5. What will it cost?

Include information in your letter about where the prospective client can contact you, and do not use mailing labels on the envelope. They give the appearance of junk mail and will only increase the chance that your letter will remain unopened and your message unread.

Brochures and Promotional Materials

Brochures and other promotional materials give the portable executives a real opportunity to convey their message in greater depth to a broader audience. These materials should be aimed at the potential customer in your market. Brochures should begin with an inspirational lead, describe the product or service in detail, offer testimonials from satisfied clients if possible, and contain concrete stories that demonstrate how the portable executive has successfully applied his or her core capabilities in real life situations.

The Design of Your Materials

The design of your brochure and promotional materials are every bit as important as your message. The portable executive must create a visual impression in the potential customer's mind. It is actually less important for the reader to remember your entire message than it is for him or her to remember seeing your brochure.

While new users of desktop publishing packages are often enthralled by the design options and typefaces they can employ, this is not the place to demonstrate what your software package is capable of doing. Every page should be visually clean, with adequate margins and simple, easy-to-read type. No more than two typefaces should be used in any one brochure and italics, bold print, and underlining should be used minimally. If you find you are relying on boldface and underlining to emphasize your point, try rewriting your copy so that it communicates your message effectively without the need for typesetting frills. Of course, your copy should be free of grammatical, spelling, and punctuation errors, as your own promotional materials are the best demonstration of your quality control. If it seems you can't handle your own quality control, chances are a potential customer will ask, "Why should I allow this portable executive to handle mine?"

You must also consider the size of your brochure and other promotional materials. Do you want a small fold-over piece that can be mailed without an envelope (which saves postage costs)? Or a glossy brochure that a potential client can't possibly resist opening? Whatever size you do choose, keep in mind that these pieces are essentially throwaways. You must remember to weigh the benefit and cost of sending them.

Direct Mail

The objective of doing a direct mailing is to get the potential client to contact you. Of course, this promotional effort should also be aimed at the potential customer, as well as those who have expressed an interest in your offering. Practically speaking, this technique is only effective if you use it consistently over a period of time.

The "Canal System" of direct mailing developed by Saatchi & Saatchi is an excellent example. In this system, you communicate with potential clients every three months for a nine-month period with a follow-up phone call approximately ten days after each mailing. Portable executive Wendy Evans has employed this system with a number of companies and says:

> **If you use this system consistently and send a believable message, people will begin to trust you. After nine months, you will see your response rate climb from one percent to three-to-four percent.**

There is absolutely no point in sending out a single direct mailing—or worse, sending one out and not following up on it.

Consistent message-sending is the key. A potential customer who receives only one mailing will wonder if the portable executive who sent it still exists in the marketplace, whereas those executives who send multiple messages in an organized manner *and* follow up on them are perceived by the potential buyer as being in the market to stay.

Newsletters

Newsletters are a terrific opportunity for the portable executive to present a message in an educational document. The technique here is to blend educational information about your industry or service with a subtle conveyance of your capabilities. Case studies and testimonial copy about your services are easy to weave into a newsletter, and since the newsletter also communicates industry information to the client, it is far more likely to be read. Portable executive Dick West, who established his own consulting company in Wichita, Kansas, found a company that provides him with a prepackaged newsletter that is relatively low in cost:

> **The company gives you an exclusive on your trade or territory—I basically have Kansas. They write an orderly newsletter, and from time to time I provide them with articles I would like to see published, usually about thirty to forty-five days in advance of publication. They send me draft copies of articles they are planning to include that quarter, and if I don't want them included, they'll delete them or use something else. It can be customized, but most of the time I use their version.**

West sends his newsletter to a target list of people he knows are buying services similar to his own from other providers, thus keeping potential clients aware that he is in the market and offering them an alternative to the services they are currently buying.

In doing this, West is following one of the basic axioms of marketing, which is to make sure that potential clients are already aware of your offering when their need to use it develops.

Advertising

As the portable executive's business develops and her budget grows, she may very well evolve to the point where the higher cost of broad market advertising is justified. Radio and TV commercials, as well as print advertisements, offer the broadest possible exposure but are usually prohibitively expensive. Another way to advertise on a smaller scale is to simply place an advertisement in the "Situations Wanted" or "Business Opportunity" section of either a major paper like the *New York Times* or a local paper, depending on the market share you're trying to reach. Again, the key here is consistency. An advertisement that appears once is almost useless, while an ad that appears regularly sends the signal that the portable executive is in the market for good.

Public Relations

Public relations can be a cost-effective way to communicate your message, but you can't always control the way that your message is going to be conveyed. Anyone who has gotten his name into a newspaper or magazine or has appeared on a TV or radio interview knows that there is no better way to make yourself known to a broad audience. With the recent expansion of local cable television and print media, more and more material is needed to fill the available time and space, creating a real opportunity for the portable executive to get exposure at a relatively low cost.

Hiring a freelance public relations consultant or publicist can help you break into these markets. Once the doors have been opened, the best way to approach your encounters with the media (and thereby maintain some control over the way the message will be sent) is to think your message through in as much detail as possible and arrive at a theme that will convey a consistently believable idea. This way, you are prepared to respond to any question asked of you with some variation of the root message you wish to send.

Consistently Convey the Message

One of the early lessons portable executives must learn is that while potential customers may in fact convert into buyers and repeat buyers at the appropriate time, they may not be ready to buy when they first hear about your product or service. These delays seldom ever have anything to do with the quality or appropriateness of your offering. Sometimes, it just isn't the "right time" for that particular customer—they either don't have a current need for the product or service or they just haven't "focused" on their need for it because they have other things on their mind. While these responses may be frustrating or discouraging, it is nonetheless very important that you continue to convey your message consistently over time to build trust and be top-of-mind when the need arises for your services.

Tracking Response Rate

Most marketing programs fail because they are not organized to keep track of the progress of individual targets—that is, when a potential customer has moved from one level of interest to another, it is critical that the portable executive respond appropriately. When a company responds to a direct-mail offering indicating that it would like more information about the product or service, that company has moved from the great unknown universe of potential clients who are "unaware" of the offering to the group of those who are now "aware." When someone indicates they are interested in having a meeting, they have moved yet another step and need to be treated accordingly.

The key to success, therefore, is to maintain control over the various levels of interest and develop a consistent strategy in dealing with each one. You can never lose sight of the fact that you are building trust and educating potential clients about your offering. By maintaining a good tracking system, you can appropriately maintain contact through newsletters or phone calls even while you are busy on other assignments. This eliminates the danger of being "out of sight, out of mind." An organized tracking system also helps you to avoid the "If you market you can't work, and if you work you can't market" dilemma.

Portable executives can handle their tracking in any number of ways, from making notes on Rolodex or index cards to purchasing a computer software package to help keep track of this information. How executives track this information is far less important than making sure that they do it in an organized manner on a consistent basis. The minimum objective is to maintain customer awareness and, hopefully, to expand it.

Focusing on Potential Customers

In developing and sending out your marketing materials, it is essential that you gauge each current or potential client's level of awareness at any given time. Imagine each client as somewhere on a continuum from "unaware of product" to "repeat customer."

In your initial efforts at marketing, you will realize that there is a very broad potential pool of customers to whom you can attempt to market your services or product. For example, much of the junk mail you receive has been aimed at the broadest possible market for a service or product being offered. You may, for instance, receive marketing materials and advertisements for every conceivable type of computer hardware and software simply because someone put you on a direct mailing list of computer owners. In other instances, the zip code you live in or your income level are the only criteria applied in targeting you as a potential buyer.

For the portable executive, however, direct-mail strategies must be focused in order to be both cost-effective and manageable. In thinking of your potential and current customers, then, it helps to assign them to one of the following categories:

1. Aware
2. Interested
3. First-time buyer
4. Repeat customer

Viewing them in this way will allow you to think about the role both you and your marketing materials need to play to move each customer from being aware to being a repeat customer.

Awareness

Creating awareness of the product or service is the first step in building a successful marketing program. While the portable executives just starting out may not have the budget to blitz the marketplace with fancy mailing pieces, they can be very effective with a small number of hand-tailored letters to a well-defined audience, with appropriate follow-up contacts. A well-designed effort that emphasizes the relevance of your product or service should produce a steady flow of interested "live" leads.

The Interested

Handling the interested population is tricky, because when potential buyers reach this level, the portable executive must respond with a careful blend of marketing and sales strategies in order to convert the interested target into an actual buyer. Handled correctly, the portable executive's response to the interested group can form the foundation for a successful sale.

In approaching potential clients in the interested group, your role is to build a relationship that enables you to tailor or adjust your offering to the clients' needs. Your approach to this group must shift subtly from that of marketing to that of sales, and you should be sensitive to the point in the relationship where this occurs. Although the line between marketing and sales is often blurred, you must continue to educate the customer about the offering even as the sale emerges and you negotiate the specifics of a particular deal. For the portable executive who wears both hats, this can be difficult, since both processes must work together in order to develop long-term customers.

The First-Time Buyer

The relationship with the first-time buyer is tenuous in nature and needs to be nurtured and developed carefully. The fact that a client is buying your service or product is a clear indication of his or her need for it, but the actual level of that need—from very slight to very great—is much more difficult to gauge. One thing, however, is certain—if you do not deliver high-quality service to the client on a timely basis, that first-time buyer will never become a repeat customer. You must therefore work conscientiously to develop a clear understanding of the buyer's expectations and be absolutely certain that you can fulfill them. The first assignment you undertake for a client sets the standard for the quality and price of future assignments. It is important that you do not compromise quality or price in your eagerness to make that first sale, as doing so either can jeopardize repeat business or attract business you do not want. Remember that the repeat customer will come back for more of what you offered in your initial dealings with him or her, and you need to be careful not to underprice your product or service and create an expectation that that price will hold throughout the relationship.

The Repeat Customer

A portable executive should always allot sufficient time in his business plans to attend to current clients and ensure that their needs are being fully met. Repeat customers form the backbone of every business, and the portable executive should never fail to recognize the need to continue to both market and sell to repeat customers. They say the best source of new business is a satisfied customer, and that should serve to remind you that your existing customers deserve more attention than anyone else.

Making Sales

In making sales—that is, persuading a particular target to actually buy your service—you must *not* agree to handle something just because it is remotely related to your core skills and you must *not* be too ready to adjust your pricing. You must have the courage to accept only those assignments that involve what you do best and maintain fair market value for your offering. Portable human resources executive Richard Achilles agrees:

> I don't want anybody to have me in a job where I have to work from my deficiencies. I'd rather have a job where I'm playing to my aces. That gives the client a better product and gives me greater satisfaction. It also means I will probably get invited back for another opportunity.

Here are some basic rules that will help you make the sale:

- Never forget that you're trying to satisfy your customer's needs and not simply trying to sell your service. Orient your inquiries and discussions to encourage clients to tell you what their needs are. As they do so, you can begin to tailor your offering to fit those needs.
- Each product or service has what is known as a "sales cycle," which simply means the time it takes to sell the offering from the first expression of interest to the time the sale is made. As you gain experience in sales, this cycle becomes very predictable. Sometimes you will make the sale on the first call, while other times a series of meetings and other contacts may be involved before the sale is made.
- People buy from people they trust. The best way for the portable executive to develop a trusting relationship with the client is to consistently deliver quality service on a timely basis at a fair price.

- You must develop good negotiating skills. Selling personal service often takes time, patience, and clear explanations to help the client understand the benefits of your offering and to convert him into a first-time buyer.
- Many salespeople fail to close the sale because they assume that if the client hesitates the interest isn't really there. You must be aware that many of the variables that impede sales have nothing to do with the offering itself and everything to do with forces at work within the company or individual one is selling to.

Ask for the Business

Last, but not least, one should always ask for the client's order. If you sense that it is truly not the right time to ask for the order, you should always walk away from a sales call with something: another meeting, an agreement to talk on the phone, or some other reason to continue the dialogue. This is, in effect, asking for the order by moving the process forward. You must also realize that while every client is somewhat resistant to being sold, they are aware that they have to buy that service from someone and that the selling process itself offers them a means of gathering information. By asking for the order, you indicate that you are interested in being a supplier or vendor, even if you are rejected on the first pass. Being rejected may not mean the customer doesn't want to buy; it may only mean the customer doesn't want to buy now.

Beware of the client who says he or she wants to buy but is in fact just shopping around or looking for bargains. For portable executives just starting out, these types of opportunities often appear attractive but usually end up going nowhere. To avoid this scenario, you should firmly fix in your mind the minimum level of commitment you expect from a client to avoid wasting valuable time. As portable executive Ed Burrell put it:

> **I get pulled into many potential business situations—and one of the challenges is sorting out which opportunities you can afford to spend your time on from the wild goose chases.**

Requesting a retainer fee will often separate those who aren't serious from the real buyers of your services.

A Final Word on Selling

Remember that your potential client is also in the business of selling a product or service and the idea of selling is certainly not foreign to him. Though it can be hard the first few times around, you should not be bashful about your offering or about reaching out to those who could benefit from it.

The sales orientation of the portable executive is based on an honest exchange of value. Any portable executive who thoroughly understands the value of his or her core skills and their possible applications should therefore go out into the market and sell them with pride.

Chapter Eleven

CLIENT SERVICE

◆

**My whole practice is one of tailoring my offerings to
what the client needs. At the same time, I think it is important to open up some focus areas. Whether I'm working for a big company, a small company, or a one-man
operation, helping the client articulate his requirements
is really key. Ultimately, you are going to be judged on
how well you meet those requirements.**

—Richard Achilles

Unlike the recent past, where unwritten organizational codes
dictated the behavior of the entire workforce, the combination of
the restructuring of American corporations and the entrance of
the portable executive into the economy has opened the door for
new, more balanced relationships to be formed. As we pointed
out in Chapter Four, however, the habits of a lifetime are hard to
break. With knowledge expanding so rapidly, all work relationships are subject to rapid change. They are flexible and assignment-oriented, creating a need for independent, balanced
relations between an organization and those who supply it with
personal services. As we will explore in the following pages,
portable executives need to operate from a new model of relationship if they are going to service clients and employers successfully.

Defining the Client Relationship

Most portable executives emerging from long-term employment relationships vividly recall the time in their lives when, if asked who they were, they responded with the name of the company they worked for and either what they did or what title they held. Today, the cachet of deriving one's identity from a large corporation with meganame recognition is fast disappearing. The "corporation man" of the past is the portable executive of the present and future, whose core attitude of self-direction defines who he or she is, and whose relationship with clients is one of trust and mutual benefit in a peer-peer exchange.

In the realm of portability, the client is an organization, person, or community to which one promises to render personal services in one's area of expertise and to complete specific projects or tasks. This definition implies certain essential characteristics that distinguish it from the now archaic lifetime employment relationship, distinctions in which the critical shift from the boss-worker relationship to a peer-peer exchange becomes clear.

"As a Full-Time Employee, I Had No Control over My Own Agenda"

The portable executive's relationship with a client is always a negotiated relationship, a mutually agreed-upon agenda. To begin with, portable executives recognize the value of their core skills and sell themselves to the client based on that value. For this reason, the portable executive has a vested interest in ensuring that his core skills are employed at an optimal level that will guarantee not only the most appropriate use of those skills, but also the best possible overall performance. Since the portable executive is, in a very real sense, only as good as the results achieved in the last assignment, he must build a reputation and attract new clients based on being able to apply his top-notch skills. He cannot allow the client to entirely dictate the terms of the assignment as the organization once did. Thus, the portable executive and the client should mutually agree on the terms of an assignment in order to guard against the inappropriate use of his core skills.

At the core of this type of negotiated relationship is a mutual appreciation between the two parties that assumes the client's high regard for the portable executive's expertise and for his professional assessment and understanding of the client's needs. Portable executive Loren Smith tells us:

> I say to my clients, "Let me ask you some questions for your own information." And usually those questions help a client identify some problems he wasn't even aware he had. Then we can talk about why certain things are happening and what could change.

Since the portable executive is strongly motivated by the challenge of the work the client has to offer, the executive who is still working within a large organization would most likely negotiate a move within the corporation to achieve a better match of his or her core skills. As Daphne Gill says:

> In middle management at AT&T, it's very easy to move around and gain more experience in different divisions, and that's more important to me than getting to the next rung.

"As an Employee, I Was Dependent on the Organization for Both My Employment Status and Career Development"

Unlike the old organizational model where executives' employment status lay solely in the hands of the organization, the portable executives recognize that they are not dependent on any one organization for their career development, success, or failure. Recognizing the flexible nature of work, the portable executive is prepared to end the client relationship when a given project or assignment has been completed and to move on to the next assignment. The relationship between a portable executive and the client can be long-term, but both parties need to review it periodically to assess whether the needs of each are being met.

These periodic reviews give both the portable executive and the client the opportunity to assess the benefits each is receiving, and to either revise the terms of their relationship or agree to end it. Bud Titsworth, a portable advertising executive, comments on the fact that in today's relationships it is not only the client who determines whether an arrangement is working:

> **Ideally, as an entrepreneur, once you have that group of core accounts or core customers, you wouldn't have to go anywhere else. These would not only be customers or clients who paid you decent money, but they would also be people you liked to do business with. One of the key advantages of working for yourself is if you're lucky and you do it right, you can choose who you work with. You don't have to work with jerks if you don't want to.**

The portable executive's core attitude of self-direction guides him or her to seek relationships that are both comfortable and challenging.

"Today, I'm a Valuable Contributor; As an Employee, I Was a Cog in a Wheel"

In the old boss-worker relationship, power emanated from the organization, and the employee derived his identity from the organization's power. In the relationship between the portable executive and her clients, the executive possesses a very clear under-standing of power residing within herself. She is an independent contributor of value from outside of the organization—as is an in-dividual who still works within a large organization—but has a portable mind-set: neither will cede their identity to the corpora-tion, nor do they perceive the corporation as giving them value. As Elaine Bednarski, a budget and personnel coordinator with AT&T, sees it:

> **I support the organization with my knowledge, and not the other way around. When I came in, I saw myself as an information service.**

The client views the portable executive as a person who is making an objective contribution to the organization in the con-text of a clearly defined project or assignment. Sometimes this blocks the effectiveness of the portable executive when he or she is viewed as not being part of the organization, but other times it allows the executive to operate in a position of relative freedom from organizational politics. In the words of portable executive Dick Swank:

> **I can look the senior lenders squarely in the eye and not mince words. If I were concerned about the future of my career at this company, I might be a bit more circum-spect.**

"Today I'm Rewarded Based on What I Achieve. As an Organizational Employee, the Reward Sys-tem Was Always Relative"

In the organization, many factors contributed to the level of employees' compensation—factors that had little to do with individual accomplishments. Factors such as longevity, status, and personality matches and clashes all influenced the reward system. For the portable executive, however, defining not only the terms of what will be achieved in any given assignment, but also the precise terms of rewards or bonuses, are part and parcel of the original assignment definition. Thus, the portable executive and the client arrive at an understanding of compensation that is based on the actual results to be achieved and not on arbitrary factors within the organization.

"Today I Focus on the Overall Needs of the Organization and Not Just My Own Discrete Function"

I'm participating in creating a business. I'm no longer a shepherd in someone else's field.

—Dave Moore

The portable executive's approach to the client is vastly different from the approach of the employee. The portable executive's main concern is with how the assignment undertaken relates to the overall good of the organization, whereas the employee tends to view his or her function in an organization as a discrete operation. The critical shift in approach here is that since portable executives operate as personal service business entities, they have a deeper appreciation of what it takes to be successful, making them more sensitive to how their assignment relates to the whole. This is more difficult to see when one is an employee with no real ownership in the business.

"As a Portable Executive, My Loyalty Is to My Work, Not to an Organization"

One of the main factors motivating the portable executive to perform so well is his dedication to delivering the highest-quality service. Since long-term job security is a thing of the past, the content and quality of work has emerged as the new basis of loyalty, which is derived from mutual support and respect between the portable executive and his clients. Manufacturing executive John Hatala describes the type of relationship one needs in order to produce an excellent product or outstanding service:

> **Whoever employs you deserves your one-hundred-percent loyalty. When you do something, do it well. Accept all the responsibilities that go with it, but don't be afraid to change.**

The Relationship with the Client

Delivering quality service to one's clients depends on a carefully integrated effort that includes a clear understanding of what the portable executive's assignment will be, adopting a responsive stance to the client at various stages of the relationship, and learning to operate within the client's organization without becoming overly embroiled in either the personalities in the work environment or the overall politics of the organization. The goal is, of course, to maintain the freedom of both parties and to use the portable executive's core skills in a way that benefits both parties optimally.

Defining the Assignment

> **The key is to ask the customer what he wants. Your customer is going to tell you what he wants and you're going to deliver it. But don't deliver something he didn't ask for. What you need to do is listen to what he wants and come up with a way to deliver it. And if you can't do it, tell him. You'll be remembered for that, too.**
>
> **—Jack Cahill**

187

Because the relationship between the portable executive and the client is oriented to the accomplishment of specific, highly defined goals and assignments, it is imperative to spell out the terms of the relationship in writing. Whether the document is formal or informal, it should include the precise tasks that are expected to be completed, estimated dates of completion for each stage of the project, and the economic terms that will apply. In hammering out an agreement of this kind, both the portable executive and the client have the opportunity to clarify the terms of the relationship and negotiate any areas of it that are unclear. The portable executive should consider it a cardinal rule to get the assignment clearly documented in this manner, since whenever the terms are not clear, the measurement of success will be equally unclear. This type of written agreement also saves both parties from having to clarify the terms in mid-assignment.

If the portable executive begins working with a client without this type of an agreement, he is putting himself at the client's mercy—especially when it comes to assessing the executive's actual accomplishments. This forces the portable executive back into the type of dependent relationship he or she has struggled so hard to avoid. Frank Purcell comments on the importance of ironing out an agreement at the outset:

> **If what you agree upon with your client is unwritten, when you come for review, he'll say, "I never asked you to do that, or I didn't know you were working on that." To the degree that you can understand exactly what the client wants done, it will make your life a lot easier.**

The Letter of Agreement with the Client

The portable executive should include the following in a letter of agreement with a client:

- A clear definition of the scope of the assignment and the results both parties expect to attain.
- A time frame for accomplishing each specific task and an estimated completion date for the assignment.
- A format that will be used by both parties to formally evaluate the progress of the assignment. For example, one might include an agreement to meet with the client once every three months.
- The basis for compensation and all inclusive elements. The letter should specify whether compensation will be based on a flat fee for the project or on a per diem rate for the time worked. In addition, the terms of any bonus arrangement for achieving specific results should be clearly spelled out. The letter should also state whether or not compensation includes a car, gas mileage, or other expenses.
- A clear definition of the portable executive's relationship with the organization's employees. It is essential that this be understood up front, as sometimes a portable executive will have the authority to make changes within the organization and implement them, while other times they may simply function as advisors. The executive also needs to know who she will be interacting with and what the basic rules governing those relationships are.
- In some assignments, the portable executive is dealing with confidential and sensitive information. In appropriate circumstances, the agreement should include a confidentiality clause and provide for indemnification for the portable executive to the same extent as for the client's full-time employees.
- A final optional clause might address whether there will be a guaranteed time frame during which the portable executive will be retained by the client. This may be important if the portable executive will be devoting her time exclusively to one client, or is assigned, for instance, to sell a company or turn one around, where the length of time allotted can often

be critical. It also allows the portable executive to plan ahead for her next assignment.

Responsiveness to the Client

Delivering quality service to one's clients involves responsiveness, or the ability to offer quick turnaround time. While responsiveness does not mean you should render your services at the drop of a hat, it does mean that you need to be in constant communication with your client. What is important is that you communicate openly about where you are with regard to your client's assignment. Following are some general guidelines that should govern your communications with clients:

- Return your client's phone calls as soon as you possibly can. If you are going to be delayed in getting back to the client, be sure to let him or her know that you are unavailable for a good reason. In the age of cellular phones and faxes, there are few excuses for not returning a client's call in a timely manner, but your availability is far less important than your ability to communicate concern for the client's situation and to be sensitive to the client's needs.
- Do everything you can to meet the dates and schedules you have agreed upon with the client. While this can sometimes be a problem for the sole practitioner with many other demands on your time, part of your responsibility as a portable executive is to determine how much work you can handle during any given time period and still deliver optimum service to each client. Of course, everyone recognizes that there are occasions when deadlines cannot be met. If this happens, the portable executive should always give the client as much warning as possible so that he can adjust for the needs of his organization. The portable executive must realize that delays in delivering services will affect others within the client's organization.
- You should also expect and demand timely client communi-

cations whenever the client is not able to meet his deadlines or give the you the support negotiated at the outset of the project. While this is harder to stay on top of, you must be in tune with the client's problems and perhaps find out when the client is unable to meet the schedule.

- You should be as quick to give bad news as you are to give good news. Also, you should not react too quickly to either bad news or good news until you're sure that the news is valid and that you understand its implications. There is always the temptation to say that something has been accomplished when it hasn't been, or to hesitate in communicating problems with a project. Just as you wouldn't expect the client to take on all of your problems, you should not attempt to take on all of the client's problems.
- Two critical components of your relationship with a client are reliability and self-sufficiency—the client needs to be able to rely on your ability to hit the ground running, to understand the problem and how to address it, and to do so without waiting for directions. An executive who is not capable of doing this is not truly portable and is merely mimicking the relationship that an organization employee has with an employer—in a sense, he is waiting for the organization (in this case, the client) to shape his course of action.

Some Reflections on Quality Control

It is critically important for every business, but particularly for the portable executive operating as a personal service business entity, to deliver the highest-quality product or service to the client. The portable executive can do a brilliant job of marketing his product or service, pricing it to attract a land-office business, and delivering it through aggressive service, but if the product or service fails to meet the client's needs, or is not as good as a competitor's offering, the relationship with the client will rapidly deteriorate.

In order to deliver quality results to the client, portable executives must have a very clear understanding of their core offering. There is often some basic confusion regarding selling a product versus selling a service. For example, lawyers and accountants often say they are in the service business when, in fact, they are delivering a product, such as a tax return or a will, to their clients. Conversely, Avon says that they are in the business of selling cosmetics, when actually they are selling a service called "home shopping with personal consultation" delivered through a basic product. Portable executives must determine precisely what their true core offering is and be prepared to convey that clearly to the client.

In a perfect world, there would be no impediment to delivering a quality product or service to the client every time. In the effort to be responsive to the client's needs and sensitive to time constraints, however, portable executives must be careful not to compromise the quality of the product or service they're delivering. They need to decide just how much they are willing to adjust their offering in response to a client's pressures. When faced with a time- or financial-pressure trade-off, portable executives need to step back and consider the fact that the assignment they are in the process of completing is a stepping-stone to the next assignment. With this perspective, it will be easier for the individual to determine which trade-offs might be acceptable to make, and which, because they will affect the balance of the portable executive's career path, are not.

Monitoring Quality

Portable executives need to develop a way of monitoring the quality of the product or service they are offering, and there is no better yardstick for monitoring quality control than a satisfied client. Part of developing sound relationships with clients is establishing an atmosphere of openness in which the portable executive invites the client's critical feedback. Learning what your clients think and feel about what you are doing is a function of the peer-peer exchange, where neither party has power or authority over the other but instead the two work together for their mutual satisfaction. While some portable executives may be reticent to ask clients for feedback for fear of criticism, it's helpful to remember that most clients are usually very open and positive about responding to such requests.

Learning from Your Mistakes

Everyone makes mistakes—but what matters when a mistake has been made is not that you're at fault but that you take the time to analyze and understand what the mistakes were and why a given project didn't work out. This is sometimes difficult to get to the bottom of, since sometimes the portable executive isn't asked back and there's no clear explanation for it. The obvious first step in this situation is to ask for feedback from the client, but it will also prove useful to talk to other portable executives to try to learn what you could have done differently.

One of the cardinal rules of being a portable executive is "Do not sell what you can't deliver," as this is often the reason behind a portable executive's failure. Again, it is essential that you sell yourself based on a current, honest assessment of your core skills and not what you wish they were or hope they become in the near future. While it is certainly acceptable to take an assignment where you are being challenged and may have to learn new ways of applying your existing core skills, it is *not* recommended that you take on a project that requires a specific core expertise that you do not possess.

Perhaps the most subtle element of quality control involves evaluating your client and determining whether he or she is someone you feel comfortable working with. It is not inappropriate to do research on a potential client, such as checking his references, before you sign on the dotted line. Plus, if the atmosphere of the client's organization is out of synch with yours, or their standards of quality are not consistent, it would be wise to reevaluate your desire for a long-term relationship with that client, just as it would be if the client makes you miserable. If your relationship with your client is basically an unhappy one, the quality of your work will be negatively affected as well.

Corporate Culture and Politics

> **When you move into a portable-executive position there are so many audiences that want to bias you. I think that is one of the hardest things to deal with—that's where you have to maintain your distance. It's tough, though, because you have to function within the culture and be sensitive to and understand how that culture is going to change.**
>
> **—Sam Marks**

Wherever you have two or more people, you have politics, and wherever people interact, there will be a corporate culture. On a relative scale, the portable executive's involvement with the corporate culture of a client's organization is limited to getting a good understanding of the personalities he or she is dealing with and a sense of how they will influence the assignment. This superficial brush with corporate politics is a very different view from that of the lifetime employee of an organization, where politics and culture are both major factors in whether one gets a promotion or advancement or even whether one can be effective in getting a job done. AT&T's human resources manager Daphne Gill put it this way:

> **When you hire consultants, it's short-term; you're paying them to get the job done . . . and you want to get everything out of them that you can; whereas with employees, it's long-term and you have to take a more humanistic role and think, "Okay, this person has been working ten-**

194

to-sixteen-hour days, and we've got to care about their physical and mental health."

While it's not always easy to fit into the culture in a client's company, portable executives should approach every assignment and every client with the attitude that they are part of the solution, not part of the problem. With this in mind, they should try to keep an open mind and be willing to experiment with new ways to achieve their goals within the various corporate cultures they encounter.

Often, the portable executive will find that portability offers unique advantages. Portable CFO Eck Vollmer remarks on his relationship as a portable executive to the politics of a client's organization:

> **I find that, coming in as a stranger, there are no politics. In every case, I've had people who are in middle management come up to me voluntarily and, after the polite introductions, say, "Hey, listen, you ought to be aware of the following. . . ." And it's amazing what information you get right up front.**

The objective viewpoint that a portable executive offers a client is generally a chief attraction as well. Consumer products executive Jack Gelman says:

> **After my first assignment, organizations that were attracted to my background started looking at me as someone who could make a difference. The reason they would offer me positions is because they perceived that they needed somebody who was different from their internal**

staff. I'm the kind of guy who comes in with a point of view, and I'm not shy about putting it on the table.

The key is to try to develop appropriately close relationships in a client's office—"appropriate" in that you should maintain a professional attitude, but you should also convey a strong sense that you are there to help make everybody's job easier.

One of the most unique attributes a portable executive brings to a client is an element of cooperation rather than competition. Since portable executives recognize the value of other people's skills, and aren't playing the political "get ahead" game, they can genuinely reach out to others in a nonthreatening way and help them see the value of working together. Enrolling the support of the client's personnel is crucial to a successful assignment.

Never forget that the client across the desk from you is a human being just like yourself. Even if he comes off as having everything under control, very often he has some problems he simply can't handle. The portable executive who understands the value of his core skills, loves to apply them to solve problems, and listens carefully to the client's concerns, is well equipped to put corporate culture issues in perspective and maintain good business relations with his clients.

Chapter Twelve

SETTING UP YOUR

BUSINESS

◆

Faced with the practical considerations of being a personal service business entity, more than one portable executive has asked: "Where on earth do I start?" Executives used to their employers handling all of the administrative elements of running a business are often initially overwhelmed by the challenge of operating their own businesses. The portable executive needs what amounts to an immediate crash course in the essentials of being a CEO. While the focus of this chapter is on how to set up your own business, all portable executives, including those who choose to return to an organization full-time, should have a thorough grasp of the complexities of running a business.

Obtaining capital, creating and managing an operating plan, identifying key advisors, selecting the appropriate structure for the business, dealing with government agencies and taxation, and providing benefits are all complicated tasks that take time away from servicing clients and developing new business. You may have the best offering in the world, but your survival depends largely on how well you are able to meet these needs on a daily basis.

Capital

The portable executive's view of capital is distinctly different from that of the lifetime employee. Capital is the fuel that drives a business's income-producing activities. Portable executives who buy products for resale, take continuing education courses to enhance their skills, hire a marketing consultant, or grant credit to a customer are making use of investments to drive their business forward. This broadened view of capital is in stark contrast to the somewhat more passive approach followed by long-term employees, whose focus is to save money for such things as their children's education, buying a house, retirement or illness. To truly become portable, you must adjust your mind-set concerning capital from a savings view to an investment orientation.

Sources of Capital

SEVERANCE PACKAGES

In the present era of downsizings, "early-retirement incentives" or "severance packages" often constitute the largest source of business capital a portable executive has at hand. Severance money is intended to cushion the blow until the executive finds his or her next position, so in a very real sense, it should be viewed as capital to fund the portable executive's business. It is a good idea to keep these funds in a separate bank account earmarked as business capital. Even when you have sufficient income and do not need to touch your severance money, learning to think of it as capital for building your business will help you set parameters around the amount of capital investment you are willing to make.

SAVINGS

The use of savings as a source of business capital should be approached with a good deal more caution. Savings serve a very different purpose in an individual's overall financial planning, so you should only tap savings after thoroughly analyzing what your savings are for and how you will replace the money you've withdrawn. To the extent that the portable executive uses savings in his or her business, a formal transfer of money should be made to the business account and interest should be charged in order to make the difference between savings and business capital clear.

VESTED PENSIONS

For many no-fault–terminated executives, the value of their pension plans is a significant asset. Depending on the particulars of the plan provided by their former employers, pension funds are available at the time of termination as a lump-sum pay out or are deferred to be tapped at normal retirement age. Since these monies are specifically designed to provide a level of support when an executive can no longer work or elects to retire, they should be safeguarded for that purpose and used only in dire emergencies.

In addition, one should not lose sight of the fact that a "qualified" pension program is a unique form of savings since contributions to it and earnings from it are tax-deferred until retirement. To the extent that it is possible, the portable executive should try to keep his or her pension "portable" as well by rolling it over into a private program such as a 401(k) or an IRA-SEP and continue to channel savings into it on a tax-deferred basis.

HOME EQUITY

Very often, the largest investment an executive has is in his or her home. Since one's home is fixed in nature and often represents relatively stable value, banks are usually comfortable lending money on a portion of the equity over the mortgage debt. Home equity borrowing may be a way for the portable executive to obtain cash relatively inexpensively. There is a catch-22 involved in using your home equity, however, because banks not only consider the equity in the home but also the income of the borrower, so it is important to secure these loans during those times when the portable executive has a job or a steady flow of income.

More than a few portable executives make the decision to sell their existing homes, use a portion of the income from the sale as business capital, and move to another location where the cost of living is lower. After portable executive Dick Swank was downsized out of Dun & Bradstreet, he looked at his home and decided:

> **I've got a big asset here, and I really don't want to incur that long-term expense of maintaining a big home. We sold our house and went up to the country where we built a house that is absolutely spectacular—for half of what we got for the other house.**

OTHER PERSONAL CREDIT VEHICLES

Using credit cards, overdraft privileges, automobile financing, and other forms of consumer credit are additional ways to maintain liquidity. While these vehicles are not designed to be used to finance a business, they can be called upon to bridge short-term needs. It is important in exercising these options, however, not to lose sight of the fact that most carry an exorbitant interest rate.

OUTSIDE SOURCES OF CAPITAL

There are a number of outside sources of business capital that may be available to you, and while many of them are only available to those whose businesses are already up and running, these sources should be included in your business plan. Types of outside capital include bank loans, SBIC (Small Business Investment Company) loans, and venture capital. You must recognize, though, that most of these capital sources are very expensive and hard to come by, despite what you may hear about them. All want a high rate of return and all expect the loans they offer to be fully collateralized and personally guaranteed. While it is hard to attract venture money for a personal service business, it can be done if you have a well-developed business plan and can show that returns are generated.

An Operating Plan That Will Grow with You

While many small businesses fail, very few do so because of lack of dedication or hard work. A poor understanding of how one's offering fits into the marketplace and lack of cash are the two most frequently cited reasons for small-business failure. For this reason, a critical factor in any portable executive's success is a solid business plan. In addition to analyzing and accounting for one's competition, and projecting costs involved in running one's business, a working business plan should also include both long- and short-term goals for the business and how they will be achieved. Everything within your business plan should flow from a solid and realistic understanding of the value of your core skills and their actual applications, not from what you would like to do with them under ideal circumstances. It is also important to set your goals within a clear time frame. One good way to approach goal setting is to categorize them as follows:

- *One-year goals.* One year goals should be very specific and short-term in scope. During the first year, you will be defining what you are going to do and formulating your plan, which should include economics, the number of clients you expect to service, and also the parameters you have set for yourself concerning tolerance for risk where your business capital is concerned. Setting a realistic first-year target is often the most critical part of the portable executive's plan, since you have to establish where the business is going in order to handle the inevitable ups and downs without becoming too discouraged.
- *Three-year goals.* Three years is probably the maximum amount of time for which the portable executive can realistically plan. A three-year plan enables you to look beyond the current year's problems and short-term targets, and is

just the right period of time to get a business up and running. A three-year plan will also help inject some reality into the process of building your business, as it offers a clear view of the steps you are taking to achieve success over time. We refer to this as the stepping-stone process in chapter six because it serves to help you focus on where you are taking your business.

- *Five-year goals.* The five-year mark is usually the place to begin envisioning the future of your personal service business entity. Long-term goals are usually too far off to be planned with any degree of certainty, but they provide a context for what can be achieved tomorrow through today's concrete actions.

In setting these long- and short-term goals and objectives, the portable executive should know that focusing too much on the here and now will create major problems for any personal service business entity, as it distracts you from expanding the business. For example, if you don't invest in the maintenance and development of your core skills and don't invest in a solid marketing campaign, you will most likely have great difficulty generating revenue. The key to good targeting is to set your long-range sights and plan each day's activities realistically to make progress toward them.

Financial Projections

Financial projections can be as simple as a home budget or as complicated as a five-year summary of earnings for the SEC. At the very least, financial projections should be cash-flow-oriented and broken down month by month in order to establish some guideposts along the way. As Carol Frenier put it, "My financial projections show me the bottom line and how the money is going to flow." While the portable executive may elect to hire an accountant or a bookkeeper to attend to these details, getting a firm grasp of your cash-flow requirements will enable you to truly appreciate the direct effect of behavior on your business.

Be careful not to become too excited about how good the numbers look. Projecting the numbers for the best and worst circumstances, then listing the actions needed to achieve the best and avoid the worst, helps ground your financial projections. Also, be slow to revise projections upward and quick to revise them downward, depending upon actual results. This will allow you to adjust for potential problems by seeking more work or cutting back on unnecessary expenses or both.

As you start your business, you'll notice how quickly cash flow begins to resemble rainfall in the High Plains. Good months will be followed by months that appear to be absolute disasters. The key to a successful business is to gradually eliminate these peaks and valleys by developing a steady flow of business that is commensurate with your overhead levels.

Getting Started

After you have defined your offering, analyzed the market, identified sources of capital, and established a solid operating plan, it is time to set a date for the "grand opening," establish your company's structure, and get a world-class office up and running. At this point, you will want to assemble a team of professionals that includes an accountant, a lawyer, an insurance agent, bankers, and other advisors to guide you through the initial processes of establishing your business. On the value of securing good start-up people, Frank Purcell says:

> **I'm a believer in going for help. It's not excessively expensive and it sure does save a lot of misery in getting set up.**

Accountants

Even if your background is in finance or accounting, one of the first relationships you should establish is with an accountant. Unlike a bookkeeper, an accountant acts as an advisor on your over-all financial situation. Be sure to interview a number of accountants, talk to people who have used them, and check their references thoroughly. You should come away from your accountant with the sense that he or she understands your business and what you want to accomplish. A good accountant should also leave you with the confidence that he or she will offer valuable practical financial advice as your business grows and matures.

While you may intuitively know more than your accountant about the economics and finances of your business, the accountant is much better trained in putting these aspects of your business into an understandable form. The ability to translate your intuitive knowledge into a recognizable form is precisely what you need in a good accountant.

Beyond the advisory aspect of your accountant's role, he or she will also be able to advise you on the multiple levels of taxation and government regulations that need to be dealt with on an ongoing basis in most businesses. Without sound financial advice in these areas, the results can be both costly and disastrous. For instance, if a business does not remit its employee's payroll taxes to the IRS on a timely basis, the owner of the business can be held personally liable for them even if the business is incorporated. If the average portable executive tried to figure out today's complex business regulatory system, he or she would have very little time to focus on actually starting the business.

Lawyers

Lawyers serve a critical function in the start-up phase of one's personal service business entity by helping the portable executive make all of the appropriate filings to qualify to do business in a state and city, and by determining what legal structure is appropriate for a given business. While you may not need a lawyer as much as an accountant once your business is running smoothly, working with one in the beginning will help you understand the various legal aspects of your business. The advice of a lawyer will prove invaluable in enforcing regulations, collecting on overdue accounts receivable, drawing up contracts with partners and clients, and forming strategic alliances. It is important to establish a relationship with a lawyer early, so that he or she gains a good understanding of your business and where you plan to go with it before any problems arise.

Insurance Agents

Many insurance agents are deeply involved with their clients' businesses. Among your basic insurance needs will be medical insurance, liability insurance, and disability insurance. In many cases a portable executive cannot become a supplier company without certain insurance policies in force. Eck Vollmer points to perhaps the most cogent reason to consult an insurance advisor:

> **What nobody thinks about is disability insurance. I would certainly recommend that portable executives look into that immediately, because a severe illness can devastate a family. Every asset you've got can go, and then you're on welfare.**

Bankers

The portable executive's relationship with her banker is as critical to the development of business as her relationship with accountants, lawyers, and insurance agents. But it is essential to devote sufficient time to educating one's banker about the business so he will feel comfortable and understand it. That way, when the need to borrow money arises, he can consider the long-term goals of your business. Even though you may not need to borrow money or even consider it, it is still important to establish some kind of credit relationship with a bank in case the need to borrow money does arise. In recent years, the banking industry has become more strict about lending money to small businesses, so it is wise for you to understand precisely what parameters your bank will set around lending money. One critical factor you must consider carefully when borrowing is the extent to which you are comfortable putting personal guarantees behind your business loans. Such guarantees expose all of your assets, so it is important to approach such agreements with the same caution you would use in deciding to tap your savings.

Benefit and Pension Advisors

One of the great advantages of working for a corporation is that the complex administration of health care benefits and pensions is usually taken care of for the employees. For the portable executive setting up a business, this can be an area of great complication and frustration. And while your accountant and insurance advisors may be able to develop a workable plan together, it often makes sense to seek the advice of a professional benefits advisor. Be sure to select someone who is compensated on a fee basis rather than by commission in order to ensure that you are getting a fair judgment.

The portable executive should look to the advisor to:
- Identify health care plans that strike a balance between routine care and catastrophic care at an affordable price.
- Prepare a comparative analysis of the coverage, approach, cost, and reliability of various health care programs.
- Advise on how best to set up a disability program.
- Advise on whether to "roll over" corporate pension plans or take immediate distribution.
- Provide a review of different programs that allow the accumulation of funds on a tax-deferred basis for retirement.

The Structure of Your Business

Among the first decisions you must make in conjunction with an accountant and a lawyer is what structure is appropriate for your business. This decision is usually driven by the type of business you are undertaking and by the tax implications involved. As a general rule, you should choose the corporate form of operations if the nature of the business could expose you to liabilities that the corporate structure would limit. Generally, businesses that sell a product or deal in a hazard service should be incorporated from the outset. In addition, any business that has more than two or three employees should be incorporated to protect you from employee-related liabilities. Sole proprietorship, partnership, and the various forms of alliances are normally chosen by portable executives who operate as consultants or interim managers, where the liability risk is small.

Tax Considerations

The structure the portable executive chooses for his or her business has a significant effect on taxes. For example, those who set themselves up in sole proprietorships or partnerships avoid all corporate taxes. If you need or want to have a corporation, forming a Sub Chapter S corporation will save you some of the tax that regular corporations are subject to. The essential difference here is that regular corporations are taxed at both the corporate and the personal level, while Sub Chapter S corporations are legally exempt from federal corporate tax and oftentimes state tax as well.

While you should rely on your accountant and lawyer for tax advice, here are a few general illustrations of the impact of taxation on the cost of doing business. Every business carries a tax cost that is usually over 50 percent of net revenues when you add up the costs of federal, state, local, income, sales, and property taxes. Consider, however, that while 50 percent of every profit dollar is paid out in taxes, every expenditure reduces those taxes by 50 percent. Therefore, you must be careful not to rationalize expenditures because of that 50 percent tax benefit, since it does not make sense to orient one's business deals solely to save taxes. The portable executive should always accept the best business deal available and worry about the taxes afterward, since you keep fifty cents for every dollar generated in revenue.

Because tax laws are not necessarily based on economic logic but rather on social policy and the need to raise revenues, you should always keep in mind that the form of a transaction, rather than the substance, can determine the tax effect. Time spent on tax planning can therefore be very valuable. For example, you should never lease employees in the state of Connecticut, because you end up paying a 6 percent "sales tax" on the total payroll. If you use a payroll-processing service instead, there is no tax.

Setting Up an Office

As the opening day of your business draws near, the question of where to set up your office must be addressed. Some portable executives like Anne Hyde find that they can comfortably operate out of home-based offices. Hyde's trick, though, is to stay in her home office all day. Once there, says Hyde, "I'm in there and I never feel tempted to go downstairs—no matter what."

Hyde, who is an early riser, starts her day by going out for breakfast and then heading back to her home office. Other portable executives feel more comfortable working away from their homes, and so they rent outside office space. It is relatively easy today to find inexpensive office space for your business that includes basic secretarial services and the shared use of fax and copying machines.

Aside from the psychological factors involved in deciding whether to work from home or outside of it, working from a home-based office offers the obvious advantage of keeping overhead expenses low. But knowing what equipment to buy and how to go about setting up an office can take time. Portable executive Jack Cahill, who also chooses to maintain his office in his home, says:

I'm using things I never ever used before—like fax machines and computers. At Unilever, there were comput-

ers everywhere. I had one on my desk, but I never used it. Now, I've taken courses and I'm computer-literate. I know how to send a fax to somebody. I had to learn things I never knew before, and it's really helped me.

Technology has brought whole worlds of knowledge to our fingertips, and the central fixture in any portable executive's office is a personal computer. The majority of executives interviewed for this book have either taught themselves how to operate computers or have enrolled in classes to learn the basics of using word-processing packages, spreadsheet software, and databases. Many portable executives also add a modem, enabling them to literally send work back and forth to clients they may never have met. Modems also allow an individual to tap into computer-user networks, small business forums, and bulletin boards, where you can talk to experts in any number of areas anywhere in the world. It's also important to join a computer network, which allows you to be contacted via E-mail (electronic mail) on your personal computer.

In addition to a personal computer (with basic word-processing, spreadsheet, accounting, and database software, and perhaps a modem), you will probably find a fax machine and a small copier helpful. Portable executive Bud Titsworth is able to share use of a copier and a fax machine with other tenants in his current office space, but if he couldn't, he says, "I'd go out and buy a fax in a minute. You can't do business today without one." The cellular phone is also fast becoming indispensable for portable executives. It represents a tremendous tool to maximize what would normally be dead time while commuting or traveling. Newer cellular phones allow the executive to send faxes and modem transmissions as well, boosting productivity even more.

Even if you're capable of handling your own correspondence, basic accounting, and other administrative tasks, it is, as we mentioned before, far more cost-effective to buy administrative services from others, thus freeing you to spend the majority of your productive time applying your core skills. It is possible to hire administrative help as needed—to send a major marketing mailing for example. Understanding how to use administrative services is important. The time will inevitably come when you have to move rapidly to service a client, so knowing how to recruit help quickly and where to find it at a moment's notice is essential.

Other items you will want to consider in setting up your business include the installation of sufficient phone lines and the availability of basic overnight and courier services such as Federal Express, Airborne Express, DHL, and UPS. Setting up business accounts with those that are appropriate and establishing relationships with vendors for office supplies, stationery, and printing needs, as well as anything else your business will require on a regular basis, is also wise. However, you should pay particular attention to setting up favorable terms with your vendors and suppliers, as will be discussed in the next chapter, "Pricing and Cost Control."

Though setting up a business requires hard work and careful planning, few portable executives would give up the freedom and control they gain in deciding how best to employ their core skills and which clients they choose to service. While there are a multitude of decisions to make at the outset—and adjustments to be made as time and circumstances change the needs of your business—becoming a personal service business entity allows you to become far better able to respond to the ever-changing needs of our global, technologically driven business community.

Chapter Thirteen

PRICING

AND COST CONTROL

◆

In a large organization, you never even realize what cash
flow is, or how it affects things. You have no understanding of the pressures and the ups and downs.

—John Trost

As a personal service business entity, the portable executive
brings a core attitude of self-direction to the economic issues of
portability. While economic reward will, to a large extent, follow
from a job well done, you need to develop a new sensitivity to
your economic situation. Long used to having an employer handle all of the day-to-day activities involved in running a business,
it may be a bit jarring to find yourself "chief executive officer,
board chairman, executive vice president, chief cook and bottle
washer, and janitor," as advertising sole proprietor Bud Titsworth
put it. Don't forget to add chief financial officer and chief marketing executive to that list, as two of the most pressing issues
you will need to contend with right from the start are how to
price your services and minimize costs.

The quality of the offering you make to your clients and your ability to fulfill the client's needs are the prime drivers of your career. What this means is that the economics are driven by the quality of your deliverables, not the reverse. Portable executives who are purely driven by economics and not by the quality of their products or services will have trouble achieving a satisfactory level of compensation over time. Therefore, the two main economic issues likely to affect a portable executive's success are pricing the offering and controlling the costs of doing business. You must attain the best possible price while maintaining the lowest possible cost consistent with rendering quality service.

Pricing

Pricing is a critical element of any business's operations—it represents what the customer is willing to pay for the assets acquired from the seller. The price that the portable executive charges not only keeps bread on the table, but also signifies return the individual receives for the investment that he has made and will continue to make in the maintenance and development of his skill set. Your skill set, as we've mentioned before, constitutes not only your prime asset, but also your entire inventory, and must be priced to generate reasonable return on your investment.

Employees of a corporation approach pricing with an entirely different mind-set than that of the portable executive. The organization sets the price for the employee in the form of the compensation level, which is affected by concerns of job security, status, perks, benefits, and even the interior design of the workplace. Longevity is also a significant factor in determining compensation for employees within corporations. And yet while all of these factors directly affect compensation, there is no measurable value assigned to them in many organizations. Compensation and, in effect, pricing within corporations, is not determined solely by an individual's accomplishments, but by the relative position of those accomplishments to other employees. Portable executives, on the other hand, tend to set their price on what specific value has been achieved by their efforts and are less governed by the relative value of others.

Pricing Strategy

For those who have had little or no experience with pricing during their careers, there are some basic, underlying elements of formulating a pricing strategy to consider. Regardless of which employment vehicle you have chosen to deliver your offering to the marketplace, your pricing strategies are rooted in your firm belief in the value of your core skills and a commitment to attain the optimum value for them.

Basis for Pricing

As you approach the development of a pricing strategy, keep in mind that compensation is a function of value given and received. Very often, individuals who are starting out as portable executives or consultants approach pricing by deciding what they want to earn rather than determining how valuable their product or service is to their clients. Portable executives must constantly test the marketplace to achieve the optimum price for their goods or services—the optimum price being the one that will generate repeat customers and offer an acceptable economic return.

In developing a pricing strategy, there are many different customs and factors that must be considered. For example, when an individual is offering a relatively standard product or service, there may be an industry custom to guide one's pricing. Certain industries, such as real estate and insurance, have fixed pricing standards, while other industries have fairly consistent pricing approaches. In the executive search field, for example, retained search firms charge an industry standard of 33 1/3 percent of an employee's first year base and bonus compensation. You can easily find what the pricing norms are for your industry by doing a little research at the library, mingling at trade associations, and networking. However, if you are offering a unique product or service, you have a great deal more flexibility in pricing and should therefore charge on the basis of the uniqueness of the value received by the customer. For instance, in the early 1980s, Eileen O'Kane drove 240 miles round-trip to the Fulton Fish Market in New York every day in order to buy fresh fish for trendy restaurants on eastern Long Island. The uniqueness of this service enabled her to achieve a price that made the effort very lucrative. Portable CFO Eck Vollmer, on the other hand, bases his pricing on the relative size of the organization:

> **Look at the size of the company . . . that's the first barometer you read. A chief financial officer of a $10 million company will be compensated at a different rate than one in a $100 million company. I take into account the difference in responsibility before I quote a fee.**

You must also be very sensitive to what your competition is charging, as the quality of your product or service gives you the opportunity to distinguish your offering from that of the competition. The added value that you bring to your clients will enable you to generate a better price. However, if you truly are a low-cost producer, you should acknowledge this by giving the customer a favorable price as long as the economic returns can be maintained.

Unbundling

Another factor that should be considered in building a price base is what costs are included in the price of the product or service and what costs are billed separately. This requires testing to see how the marketplace reacts. For instance, some clients will readily pay for itemized add-on costs like travel or printing but would react negatively if you raised your prices and included—

but did not identify—these costs. For instance, John Trost, who has a market research business, bills for computer tabulation costs (which can be clearly identified in terms of time and reports delivered) separately from qualitative research hours. Identifying your costs in this way enables you to avoid being perceived as having unjustifiable price differentials by the marketplace.

Pricing as Your Business Grows

One of the most gratifying factors that can influence the basis for pricing is to become so busy that you've reached the limits of your capacity and can't keep up with the workload. In terms of pricing, it is appropriate at this point to raise your prices as you become more selective in the types of assignments and clients you choose. For instance, marketing consultant Jim Schwarz focuses on rendering in-depth service to a few clients at what he terms "a very favorable price," rather than taking every piece of business that comes along, which he feels creates "an overhead monster that must be fed."

Methods of Pricing

VALUE PRICING

While the most appropriate and perhaps purest way for you to price your service or product is to determine the real value it adds to the client's business, it is often very difficult to come up with true value pricing. There are, however, several techniques that you can use to determine a price that reflects the value of the services you render.

One possible approach is to suggest a combination of a base fee and a large incentive payment or bonus payment based on achievement. For this strategy to be effective, you *must* negotiate the exact measure of achievement in writing in advance. When the benchmarks used to measure results are clearly understood and agreed to by both parties in advance, it is less likely that there will be arguments at the end of an assignment concerning whether a bonus or incentive has been earned.

Another way the portable executive can arrive at a value-pricing strategy is through analyzing the pricing policies of the competition for similar services. When you look at the pricing schedules of large consulting firms offering the same services, you'll see that their pricing structures are often significantly higher than those of smaller firms. While these higher fees are often based on the firm's ability to offer a broader range of services, you must realize that those higher prices often include overhead costs that you as a sole practitioner do not have. In comparing pricing structures, then, you should strive to come up with a price that includes the value portion of that large consulting firm's pricing structure but not the overhead expense. Clients often perceive that they are getting unique value for the price they are paying when you employ this strategy, particularly because you are a small personal service business entity. Advertising executive Bud Titsworth remarked on this phenomenon:

> I can't quantify this for you, but I have a strong sense that a lot of my clients like me and my organization because nobody else knows about it. They like that I am this little one-man band doing business with some great big huge companies.

FORMULA PRICING

Most individual portable executives should calculate a standard price formula as a guide for quoting prices to clients. Following is a relatively simple example of one approach.

Normal hours available per year:	2,080 (40 hours a week x 52 weeks)
Percentage that is billable:	50%

Actual client hours:	1,040
Cost Elements:	
Overhead costs	$50,000
Targeted pretax earnings	$100,000
Total Cost & Profit:	$150,000
Hourly Rate: ($150,000 / 1,040)	$144 per hour

It should be noted that for formula-pricing purposes the general rule among consultants is that they will average 50 percent of their available time on income-producing client assignments (i.e., billable hours). While formula pricing does not represent the actual value that the client is receiving, it does help you to set a standard for what you're seeking to achieve. For example, financial consultant Dick West charges $150 per hour for everything he does. As he explains:

> **When I'm doing clerical work, I guess you could say that the client gets hit pretty hard, but I figure, with my experience, my time is worth $250 an hour, so at $150 everything pretty much balances out.**

As with any formula approach, the balance among down time, productive time, and overhead cost varies and needs to be monitored closely over time.

HYBRID PRICING

Hybrid pricing is a combination of value pricing and formula pricing that employs formula pricing for the basic "bread and butter" assignments and value pricing for those projects that truly contain added value. Most successful portable executives who operate as consultants focus on developing enough fee-for-service retainers to cover their basic overhead, allowing them the flexibility to take on riskier projects that offer the potential for value payoffs.

"WHAT THE TRAFFIC WILL BEAR" APPROACH TO PRICING

Deciding to charge whatever the traffic will bear is probably the least recommended form of pricing, but it is often employed by those who are either just starting out or trying to break into a new market. With this approach, the portable executive becomes dependent on pricing to obtain assignments, and is therefore not necessarily conveying the full value of the skills he or she is selling. At close examination, this approach creates an employer-employee relationship model that is not unlike that of the employee within an organization. This approach should be used very cautiously, since it can keep you from ever realizing the real value of your offering.

Discounting

You can create a wonderful pricing system that reflects the value of the products or services rendered to the client and then lose it through a loose or uncontrolled discounting policy. First consider the types of discounts you are willing to give and then calculate the probable impact of discounting on your pricing. Some of the types of discounting are:

- *Volume discounts.* Most businesses are willing to give lower prices to their customers based on a high volume of business. In granting these kinds of discounts, it is important that you base them only on the actual volume and the continuation of that volume. High-volume discounts should not be granted just because a client's volume peaks. Regardless of the situation, the portable executive must establish policy around volume discounts very clearly.
- Another form of discounting is the *retainer relationship*, often used by individual consultants or interim managers. This type of discount grants the client a lower price in exchange for a guaranteed fee over a specific period of time. This is an important stabilizing factor in the development of a portable executive's business, but you need to establish pre-

cisely what the retainer covers and be prepared to charge separately for those services not included in the scope of the retainer agreement.

- *Seasonal discounting* is another important pricing factor, in that it allows you to maintain continuity and also absorb overhead during an off season. You must be careful, however, that it doesn't become a permanent part of your pricing structure, which will erode your margins.
- *Barter exchange* is another form of discounting that can be instrumental in building your business. The most common barter exchange consists of specialist services for office space and office services. Bud Titsworth, who started as a portable executive in 1980, has never paid any cash for rent, but has always had an office on barter terms with a client.

Cost Control

Rather than employ the philosophy of "a penny saved is a penny earned," the portable executive would be wise to subscribe to the practice of "a penny well spent is a penny earned." As you approach the question of how to spend money well in a personal service business entity, there are two basic types of spending that you need to understand: expenses and investments. Both require an outlay of money, but one generates an economic return while the other does not.

Expenses and Investments

Expenses are costs that generally do not have a direct effect on generating revenue, though they may offer indirect value and are vital to your business in that respect. Expense items include communications costs, accounting, legal and other professional services, and office supplies.

Investments, on the other hand, are those expenditures that directly effect revenues. Investments include the cost of sales trips to close deals, sample products or services that you distribute to clients, and direct marketing or advertising costs.

It is often difficult to determine whether an expense is an investment, but what is important is that you understand that both expenses and investments serve a valid function and need to be monitored separately. As a general rule, expenses should be kept to a minimum and consistent with the support required, while investments should be gauged according to the likelihood of a return within a reasonable period of time, usually one year. For instance, if a direct-mail campaign does not show measurable results in a year, you should reexamine it for effectiveness.

Every portable executive makes capital investments, and it is appropriate to view the return on these investments over a three-to-five-year period of time. Capital investments include computers, office furniture, a fax machine, etc., and the key to balancing these types of expenditures lies in measuring the returns that each generates.

Elements of Cost Control

The smartest thing that any portable executive can do is to work out a cost-control strategy that includes the basic expense and investment expenditures incurred on a daily basis. Many things can be done inexpensively without sacrificing effectiveness or quality. You don't need to do *everything* first-class, however it may make sense to spend more on activities that have a direct impact on developing new business. For instance, you can choose to take the subway or bus rather than a cab to meet a client for lunch, and then spend a little more in going to a nice restaurant.

Develop an Expense Budget

Every portable executive, regardless of the type of employment vehicle chosen, should develop an expense budget and try to live by it. The budget should be broken down into expense and investment categories so that you can consider each expenditure in light of the return realized. It is also important to track your fixed and variable costs. Fixed costs are those you pay whether you are earning income or not, while variable costs are those that depend on income, such as the cost of extra administrative support during an extraordinarily busy business period.

Outsourcing

Not only does outsourcing allow you to make the best possible use of your time, it can also be far more cost-effective to outsource certain activities to others. You should be on the lookout for services that can be obtained through bartering with individuals who also need your skills in their businesses. For example, a portable executive in marketing might barter the development of promotional materials for an accountant in exchange for accounting services. With many more contract workers and portable executives in the marketplace, this has become much easier to do.

The Effect of Time on Cost

The portable executive should be aware of the ways that time and cost relate, and make appropriate decisions about when extra costs are justified. For example, most companies charge a premium for expedited services, so a decision must be made as to when such premiums are appropriate. It is much more costly to send a letter overnight than by two-day guaranteed mail through the post office. Part of the portable executive's plan for cost-control should therefore include the development of criteria for incurring these extra expenses.

Cash Versus Costs

The most important thing to remember in starting life as a personal service business entity is that "cash is king." Everyday financial decisions will flow from this principal and should always be directed toward the preservation and generation of cash flow.

Cash flow is a far more critical issue for the portable executive than for the "lifetime employee," since the lifetime employee's regular paycheck guarantees a predictable level of cash flow. The portable executive needs to plan for the erratic ebb and flow of cash that results from not always being able to predict when one will have assignments or how much cash each assignment will generate in any given period. The portable executive must therefore distinguish between cash and costs in analyzing his or her financial position. Cost is what you ultimately pay to acquire goods and services, while cash flow is what you pay in real dollars.

In balancing cash and cost, the portable executive needs to understand the use of credit, and although he or she has undoubtedly used credit before, the principals at work in using credit for one's business are somewhat different than those for personal use. Business credit revolves around "granting" credit to your clients while at the same time "getting" credit from your vendors. The trick is in learning how to balance giving and getting credit in order to maximize your cash flow. Below are some of the more typical ways that you can achieve this balance.

Handling Receivables

When dealing with customers or clients, you should always attempt to get cash payments as close to the actual delivery date as possible. To facilitate this, be sure to:

- Always bill the customer or client promptly. Most clients have a time lag before processing invoices from vendors, so the sooner that you get the invoice to the client, the sooner they will get it processed and paid.
- Establish payment arrangements with the client so cash flow will be predictable. This often takes the form of a retainer arrangement where you and the client know that you are going to do a certain amount of work over a period of time and you then receive regular periodic payments. This cuts down the work for both of you.

- Always receive advance payments for monies you will have to lay out on behalf of the client. This is very common in the advertising field or where you are rendering a service as an agent for a client. You should establish the fact that the client will make these advances as a matter of course.
- Grant reasonable cash discounts for prompt payment. If the industry has standard terms for payment, you might be able to vary those standards by granting specific cash discounts for payments made early. For example, you may offer a 3 percent discount in exchange for ten day net payment terms.
- Follow up on late receivables immediately. Even though clients may agree to the payment terms, there are always some who are consistently late. Some companies just expect to be dunned, so don't be bashful about doing so, since they are, in effect, using you as a source of credit.

Credit Cards

Portable executives should try to obtain the largest credit lines they can, preferably while they are still employed full-time, so that those lines can be tapped in a cash-flow crunch. Credit cards, of course, carry one obvious disadvantage: at an 11 to 21 percent interest rate, this is probably the most expensive way to cover a cash-flow problem unless you use them only for a thirty-day float and pay the balances in full.

Leasing Versus Buying

In many instances, leasing offers a way to conserve cash. Cars, computers, and other big-ticket items can be leased, saving you from having to lay out cash up front. The decision about whether to lease or buy, however, should be weighed very carefully, as there are instances when the cost of leasing outweighs the benefits. An accountant can help you figure out what the true cost of leasing, as opposed to buying, actually is.

Dealing with Suppliers

Just as your clients will attempt to use you as a credit-granting agency, so, too, should you negotiate with vendors and suppliers for the best possible terms. These arrangements will help to offset cash-flow problems created while you wait for receivables to be paid. As you will quickly learn, there are very sophisticated credit-monitoring agencies that furnish your suppliers with reports on your payment patterns. It is therefore important to maintain a consistent record of payments to be able to use credit.

When acquiring goods and services for inventory, one can often work out deals with vendors and suppliers to deliver the goods "just in time," so that the need to carry inventory is eliminated. Large companies are doing this more and more, and portable executives who buy inventory should use this strategy where appropriate.

Fine-tuning

Finally, while your pricing strategy should remain fairly consistent and your cost-control measures should be well thought out in advance, both areas will need continual fine-tuning to achieve your economic goals over a lifetime. While the need to continually strike and restrike these balances to maximize profit margins may initially involve a great deal of anxiety, like all of the other risks you take, the rewards that come with controlling these aspects often outweigh the experience of working as an employee of a large organization.

Chapter Fourteen

PORTABLE,
AND LOVING IT

◆

It's one thing to talk about the attributes of portability; it's quite another to practice them over a lifetime. The personal and the professional transformations you will undergo in becoming truly portable involve a deep commitment to being self-directed in every aspect of your life. At times, the road to portability may be tough to negotiate, but once you have accomplished the essential transition, your possibilities in the marketplace are limited only by your imagination. In this chapter, we will take an in-depth look at five individuals who adopted the core attributes of portability, and whose lives now illustrate how the consummate portable executive operates in today's rapidly changing workplace.

A Banker Goes Portable in the Nonprofit Sector

"The notion of becoming a banker was always preeminent in my mind," says forty-five-year old former banker Keith Darcy, looking back at the early part of his career. A third-generation banker whose own career path had followed a straight uphill trajectory that took him from a position as head of the Westchester/Rockland Division of Marine Midland Bank to a position in which he acted as CEO for a joint venture between Frank B. Hall & Company and the General Reinsurance Corporation, then back to Marine Midland, where he worked on a major strategic assignment and reported to the vice-chairman. Eventually, a combination of personal growth and restlessness led Darcy to leave banking and major organizations altogether.

Sitting on a beautiful sandy beach on the Hawaiian island of Kauai with his family in August 1989, Darcy began asking himself some important questions:

> First, I asked myself, "Do you want to be a banker for the rest of your life?" and I said, "Nope." Then I asked, "What is it that you want to do?" I wasn't quite certain at the time, but there were four powerful experiences coming together in my life: my realization that I had real power in the executive suite, and how important it was to me that I exercise that power responsibly; my experiences teaching as a faculty member at various universities for almost twenty years, which I very much enjoyed; the executive-development aspects of my work, where I saw that with an appropriate investment in education I could create a sense of aliveness for people in mid-career whose work lives felt as dead as mine did; and my involvement in Republican politics at the local, state, and national levels.

There, on the beach, Darcy recalled a quote of the Presbyterian minister Frederick Buechner's that continues to be meaningful to him to this day: "We are called to the place where our deep joy meets the world's deep hunger." The day he read it, says Darcy, "I began to figure out where my deep joy was and where my talents and my skills and my experience could best be applied elsewhere." No stranger to major life changes, Keith Darcy decided on his fortieth birthday to go back to school to earn a master of divinity degree, and managed to be "a banker by day and a seminarian by night."

In January 1990, Darcy realized that what he really wanted to do was to start an institute for ethics and leadership. When he returned to the bank, he basically sought to eliminate his own job and negotiate an exit package so that he could start his own foundation. The bank agreed to pay him two year's salary if he agreed to stay for one more year, thus giving Darcy a two-year head start.

On his first morning at home Darcy recalls his twelve-year-old son Timothy asking, "Dad, if you're not in charge of the eighth, ninth, and tenth floors anymore, who are you?" As prepared as Keith Darcy thought he was for his transition, both he and his family members went through a collective identity crisis once he left the bank, in part because they all had to come to terms with the loss of status that accompanied Darcy's decision to quit his position as a prominent banker.

> Timothy went through an identity crisis and my wife Lynne went through an identity crisis. She was no longer the wife of a successful banker. And so there was a part of me in the first month or two or three at least, where I got up and did research toward the work I intended to do, but there was a part of me that felt lost. I wasn't quite sure how to go about it or where to go with it. There was a part of me that felt unaccomplished. I didn't have the old crutches to fall back on. I didn't have the infrastructure—a system of people who support the work that you do—beneath me. For a number of months, despite making progress toward some as yet unforeseen goal, there was a big part of me that suffered tremendous anxiety.

Darcy planned to model his ethics and leadership institute after the Aspen Institute in Colorado. As he moved forward, however, he realized that he couldn't possibly bring together the entire comprehensive model he had envisioned because it would demand far more capital and capacity than his personal service business entity possessed. In that initial planning phase, Keith Darcy lost what he estimates to be between twelve to eighteen months of his time, but he adds, "In hindsight, I might also say that gave me a time to grow and learn the subject matter I'm now dedicated to."

The realities of generating revenue helped Darcy to focus on a slice of his original model—consulting and training in ethics and leadership for corporations. Today, after two years of focusing on building that one aspect of his plan into a viable business, Keith Darcy is finding that ideas from his original, comprehensive model are beginning to reemerge, and he realizes that the future growth of his company will probably depend on developing strategic alliances with other portable executives to incorporate other facets of his plan into the business:

> I never really stopped nurturing some of the other pieces [of the plan] that can probably still be developed. At first, I was not able to attend to them—I had to prioritize. But I was able to incorporate at least some of the essence of those other pieces into the business, and I can probably still develop them in alliance with other people, just not by myself. So if I meet someone with an interest or an expertise that somehow fits in with a particular part of the plan, I immediately think, "Maybe there's a way to form an alliance."

Looking back, Keith Darcy admits that in the early part of his career he was dependent upon the organization in the sense that he had a compulsive need to take care of the bank's needs as if it were "the great parent of all." "I became dependent on it," says

Darcy, "until I was able, through a sense of brokenness, to let go." Today, Darcy says:

> **I have found that I have become increasingly confident in what it is that I have to offer the rest of the world. I approach other people as a whole person, and what they think of me is irrelevant to what I think about myself, because now I feel whole.**

Multiple Employment Vehicles, One Career

Executive search consultant Anne Hyde left England and came to the United States in the late 1960s, and for two and a half years worked with management consultants. From there, she moved to the Ted Bates Advertising agency, where she worked on new business development and market research, and then, subtly shifting her core skills, she moved to *Previews*, where she and a colleague ran a division of the company marketing second homes.

At the same time, several events in Hyde's life pushed her in the direction of becoming a portable executive. Her mother, the last remaining member of her family, died, and Hyde herself became ill and bedridden for six months. She kept herself going by envisioning what she wanted to do with her life, and eventually how she could start her own business.

Realizing that she had enough money to survive for two years if she lived very simply, Hyde decided to leave *Previews* and start thinking about starting her own company. That summer, she met up with someone she'd met before, Janet Jones-Parker, who had been a manager at TWA responsible for implementing change and increasing productivity and efficiency for all of their flight attendants, and the two decided to become partners. Jones-Parker had a friend with an M.B.A. from Harvard who served as their business advisor. He advised that the two should try to address the needs that recent legislation on hiring women had created for corporations. "What we didn't know at the time," says Hyde, "is that what he was talking about was a female-based executive search firm." Starting with $6,000, Hyde and Jones-Parker were lucky enough to find inexpensive office space in New York's Plaza Hotel, which as Hyde points out, "was a good way to start, because people don't forget you." Hyde did her own cash-flow projections for the business and found at the end of six months that they were only $100 off her original projections. Soon, their business had gained national prominence, and with three consultants and support staff members they moved into the Galleria on East Fifty-seventh Street. As they grew more prosperous, Hyde found herself spending most of her time managing her managers and realized that she'd gotten away from the research work she liked most.

After the first year in business, Hyde realized that if they wanted to play in the upper leagues they'd have to shift from being a contingency operation to being a retainer search firm. Hyde's reasoning was that, as a contingency operation, they only made money when they made a placement, whereas as a retainer search firm, they'd work with senior-level executives, and, as a result of the different fee structure, gain the time to do national searches. Soon, Anne Hyde and her partner had carved out an enviable position for themselves as niche players in a market where the demand for their services was tremendous.

Then in 1980, another company offered to acquire them, and Hyde and Jones-Parker went along. Soon, however, the two decided it was a disastrous move and decided to buy the company back. They assumed a great deal of debt, and everything they owned was put up to collateralize the loan. Then Jones-Parker suddenly became ill with hepatitis, and Anne Hyde was left with sole responsibility for the business. Though terrified, Hyde determined to stick it out. She eventually took on a potential partner, but he didn't work out and Hyde again took sole command of the company. When the chairman of MSL International asked Hyde to join them, she was ready to go back to the organization:

PORTABLE, AND LOVING IT

> By this time, I was burnt out . . . totally and completely,
> I was a moron, a zombie. I was emotionally, physically,
> and in every other way burnt out. I thought, "How won-
> derful for somebody to look after me and all I'll do is
> work and draw my pay." So I did a very foolish thing, in
> a way, but in a way it was a very good thing. I joined
> them. I closed my company down, and I will never ever
> forget standing in that office waiting to hand the key to
> the next tenant. For a long time, I couldn't even drive
> past my old office, because I felt I had failed myself.

For a year and a half, Anne Hyde thrived at MSL, but then the
corporate life again became problematic:

> I found the bureaucracy more than I could stand, and I
> drove them crazy. I had become very self-sufficient. I
> was a one-man band, and I went out after business and
> didn't rely on other people to bail me out. I didn't dele-
> gate. That drove the office manager crazy, and he de-
> cided that I wasn't a team player. That's true. I didn't like
> waiting for permission. I didn't like asking if I
> should. . . . I saw opportunity, and I said, "For God's
> sake, let's go after it," but by the time I would get per-
> mission, it was gone. So I got chastised a number of
> times, and in the end I decided it wasn't worth it.

Once again, Hyde went out on her own. She analyzed her cash
position and figured out the number of searches she would need
to do to cover her projected expenses. This time, Hyde was far
more pragmatic about how she went about planning things, because she knew she didn't want the pressure of having to meet a
huge quota. "It was very scary," says Hyde, "but my need to con-

trol, to develop my own life, was more important to me than the fear that maybe I might fail again."

Today, Anne Hyde runs her new and expanding company, the Hyde Group, from a home-based office, and her group of researchers are retained as and when needed. Her own experience with bureaucracy has resulted in the attitude she now takes with them:

> **I always say to my researchers, "We're partners. You have to know as much about what is going on as I do. You'll know the results of every meeting that I have with a client."**

The Hyde Group's business has diversified its services. In what Hyde terms "the flip side of recruiting," she has found another niche market—assisting employees in moving their careers through the maze of reorganizations and restructurings, and redeploying themselves in the workforce. Today, she combines both executive search and leadership coaching. Anne Hyde has managed to operate as a portable executive by adjusting the employment vehicles she chose to use to deliver her services to the market. The career she has built for herself has been modular in nature and as flexible as both she and the market conditions affecting her business needed it to be.

A Fortune *100 Executive Goes Portable*

"We're living in the era of the one-day renewable contract," says Mike Hostage, an executive whose route to portability has included building or acquiring four businesses with his children and other members of his family. After receiving his M.B.A. from Cornell University in 1955, Mike Hostage went to work for Procter & Gamble, where, he says, "It was a given that I would be there for the rest of my life. We'd even picked out the suburb in

Cincinnati where we would someday move." Eight and a half years later, when Hostage left Procter & Gamble for the Marriott Corporation, he left, "loving the company in a way I thought I never would again. I thought when I went with Marriott it would never be the same, but I developed the same feelings about Marriott."

In the thirty-one years that Mike Hostage spent as an organization employee, he rocketed to the top of corporate America, first as the executive vice president and "de facto chief operating officer" of the Marriott Corporation, then as chairman of the Continental Baking Company, a division of ITT, and then in 1982 as chairman of the Howard Johnson Company. Hostage's parachute monies from Howard Johnson, coupled with his family's desire to stay in the Boston area, led him to become sensitive to the opportunities for small businesses.

Throughout his career, Mike Hostage had "always looked at entrepreneurs and wondered if I could have been successful at what they were doing." When he left Howard Johnson, he rented an office, realizing as many emerging portable executives have, that "nothing was going to happen unless I made it happen." Over the next year, Hostage, who has ten children with his wife Dot, began to look at a variety of business options with the definite idea that he would go into business with at least some of his children. At the same time, he got into the real-estate development business, of which he says:

> **Thank God I wasn't successful at it, because if I had opened any one of the three or four hotels I tried to develop just before the late-eighties "depression" began, I would have lost my shirt.**

Four businesses eventually evolved from Mike Hostage's entrepreneurial spirit. Today, with one of his sons in Boston, he runs Hamilton American Speedy Printing, which is a franchise of a second company Hostage owns, the New England Franchise Corporation, the master franchisor for American Speedy Printing in New England and New York State. Hostage also owns a check-cashing company, TYD, Inc. (for "Thank You Dad!") with another son in Washington, D.C., as well as a commercial nursery in Florida with his sister. Despite all of his previous career success, however, Mike Hostage experienced a number of challenges in the early days of getting his companies up and running:

> One of the mistakes I made was doing too many start-ups at the same time. For two or three years, it was pretty tense. When you have your own money on the line, you definitely have a different attitude. Today, I would have attempted to sequence those businesses.

During those few tense years, Hostage experienced his share of sleepless nights, but at the height of one problem in particular, he made a decision that became an organizing principle for all of his businesses and helped solve the initial problems with one in particular:

> I resolved that if anything was going to go under, it would go under because someone else took it away from me and not because I gave it up. I resolved that I was not going to my grave thinking I had quit something that in another month or six months or with another bright idea might have been fixed. Once I made the decision that I wasn't going to quit, it narrowed the range of things I needed to worry about.

Mike Hostage also realized during this period that his "*big-business hands-off mode*" of running a business was not appropriate. Today, Hostage says that he would find it difficult to go back to work for a large organization, but that if he ever did, "I would manage it on a hands-on basis the way you do a small company and probably do a better job of it."

With the exception of one son who is an Air Force colonel, Mike Hostage's ten children are *all* entrepreneurs. Hostage explains:

> **My children were all brought up in an environment where once you were out of college you worked for a big company—that's just what you did. Small business wasn't anywhere in our lives. But none of them wanted to go into big business. I thank God this happened, because the corporate life I found coming out of college just isn't there anymore. Careers today are very much more self-directed. Loyalty is much thinner. Companies regard you for your skill. Today's usable skill. I could handle that today if I were back in big business, but I couldn't have handled it then. It's completely different for me today. The definition in those days would have started with "I relate to the company." Now it starts with "these activities relate to me."**

Multiple Applications of Core Skills

Marketing-communications portable executive Dusty Bricker has carved out a niche for herself putting together world-class events, corporate promotions, and sponsorships on a senior-management level. Earlier in her career, she moved from one corporation to the next, creating new programs from scratch, or launching promotional events. As Bricker observed:

> **I've always called myself an "intrapreneur," meaning I would work in very large corporations and yet carve out**

niches for myself that weren't necessarily defined when I got there.

After Bricker returned from Hong Kong, where she created a target media business for the international group of *Time* magazine, she stayed with the company as a consultant to the publisher of *Fortune,* putting together issue-oriented conferences. After two and half years, she had positioned herself to work with CEOs and senior management and had developed an excellent network of contacts. But when she actually did go out on her own, Bricker experienced some anxiety about the lack of a regular paycheck.

> **I am completely responsible for my own financial success now, and the type of consulting I'd done for the first year was mostly project-oriented. At the same time that I'm working and dedicating myself to business, I'm thinking, "What's around the bend, and where is my next client going to come from?"**

Though Bricker went about building her business around her core expertise in staging world-class events, she did realize that "there are just so many world-class events, and that may or may not pay the rent, so there has to be some flexibility toward other areas of bringing in revenue." Her solution was to balance her business with other standard public-relations and marketing consulting services until the day comes when she has built her reputation and can say, "I am only going to do world-class events." The key to Bricker's success has been her ability to recognize that what she did for one company as an employee she could offer to multiple clients as a portable executive.

Moonlighting the Way to Portability

Fifty-three-year-old human resources executive Paul Upham is a seasoned veteran of the "corporate wars" of downsizing in America. As an organizational employee he was no-fault–terminated by both American Cyanamid and Donnelley Marketing. Commenting on the old notion of lifetime employment, Upham is quick to say:

> **For most people, with the exception of those like Tom Watson, Jr., it never existed. You can have a great working relationship in the best sense of the term with a boss or a subordinate or a peer on a personal basis, but forget about it on a business basis.**

Initially, Upham found his search for a new position difficult, but when he took on an interim assignment for a company in Chicago, he began to see that the life of a portable executive could be attractive. In an unusual arrangement, Upham had already done fifteen years worth of consulting work on the side with the full permission of his employers.

> **It was fun. In those days I would have done it for free because it kept me in touch with other types of industries, people, and businesses.**

So when Upham thought about a portable career, he already had a business registration, a letterhead, and cards for the company he'd formed around those moonlighting assignments. Among his first assignments as a portable executive was a stint at General Motors—a long-time moonlighting client—doing succession planning, and then he was hired by a small dry-cleaning-business owner to do organizational development.

Unlike during his early days of moonlighting, Paul Upham the portable executive decided to form a strategic alliance with another executive to make the sales. Once they've made the sale, it is one of Upham's first considerations to sit down with the client and find out what he or she expects from the relationship:

> I'll say, "What do you expect out of human resources on a long-term basis? Do you want me to be the guy who follows the elephants with a broom and dustpan? Do you want me to be a business partner who strategically integrates with your top management team and is one of the advisors?" Often the client doesn't know, so I say, "Let's think this through and talk through it because its important to me to know what your needs are and how I can best meet them."

Upham finds there's a huge difference between the way you are treated when you're an employee and how you're treated as a portable executive or consultant:

> As it says in the Old Testament, "a prophet is not honored in his own country"—that's how it is when you're an employee, no matter what level you're at. When you're a consultant, it seems that you have instant credibility until you screw up.

Though Paul Upham continues to plan for the growth of his own business, he would not turn down another position within a corporation. A self-described "corporate gypsy" and a "survivor," Upham believes that everyone has a skill or a talent they can sell.

You are the resource, and it's up to you to figure out what it is you have that's marketable. There's a message in the Parable of the Talents that transcends Christianity. It says, "Hey we all have something." Identify what that something is and you can bet that somewhere there's a market for it.

All five of the executives profiled in this chapter have taken the time to identify their talents. They've experimented with and discovered the various new ways that they can apply those capabilities and attributes, and they've sought and found the corresponding need in the marketplace for what they do best. Self-directed, they are not waiting for someone else to come along and make something happen in their work lives. They act out of their belief in themselves and their talents, and consequently they know both the exhilarating freedoms and the responsibilities of being portable. For these five people, and in fact for all executives who make the transition to portability, the organization—in whatever guise they meet it—is merely an employment vehicle. Portable executives *are* their own business entities, no matter where they happen to be working. And whether the constant waves of restructuring in this country, are, as we contend, structural changes in our economy, or, as some still hope, cyclical ones, the bottom line for those who truly embrace portability is that downsizing has forever lost its sting.

Epilogue

THE PORTABLE

ORGANIZATION

◆

The thinking about downsizing in the past was always, "We'll be downsized, then we'll shape up and move on from there." Now the market is driving for efficiency, technology is causing continuous change, the product-line cycle is lasting no more than a year. So the idea of constantly reshaping your workforce and structuring and restructuring is no longer crisis management—it's continuous day-to-day activity.

—Pete Townley

This book is meant to serve as a guide for individual executives coming to terms with the new age of portability, but the subject would not be complete without a look at how the issues of portability affect organizations. As Pete Townley's quote suggests, downsizing and restructuring now appear to be permanent features of the marketplace, and both the individual and the organization have a long way to go in working out the practical issues involved in an increasingly flexible, portable workforce.

Though organizations originally triggered the growth of the

portable work force by eliminating the promise of lifetime employment, their ability to assimilate portable executives as a permanent part of the work culture is taking somewhat longer. It is
not unusual for institutions to move more slowly to reflect structural changes in the environment, but it is important to understand that progress is being made toward accommodating
portable executives. The issues that still need to be worked out
are becoming clearer every day.

There is a growing acknowledgment by both individuals and
organizations that there is no longer any such thing as permanent
employment. As Joe Walker, the CEO of CTS, Inc., a New York
Stock Exchange electronics manufacturer, puts it, "We have no
more permanent employees. We just have longer-term employment arrangements." The recognition that a dramatic shift has
taken place in the way we all think about work is opening the
lines of communication between employers and their employees.
They're beginning to talk about what the limits of a job are, what
is expected to be accomplished through a particular job or project, and how the reward system will recognize the contributions
of a flexible workforce.

Training—actually, cross-training—within the organization is
becoming intensely focused on the development of multiple
skills to better prepare an employee to move from one in-house
assignment to the next, thereby prolonging an individual's employment period within a single organization. Organizations, in
conjunction with outplacement firms, are also getting better at
helping managers accept the exit process when jobs or assignments come to an end.

While power often still remains with the employer, subtle
shifts toward a more egalitarian peer-peer relationship are beginning to occur. Little things, like flexible work hours (to accommodate employees' other commitments), paternity leave time (so
fathers can also spend quality time with their children), "dress
down" days (which offer a break from the daily uniform), or, in
some companies, "dress up" days (for when a customer comes to

call), may seem unimportant but are actually significant in that they recognize the individuality of those who have come together for a common cause: the organization.

On a broader scale, the current trend toward "reengineering" the organization testifies to the fact that knowledge is the main component of all goods and services. While reengineering focuses on the processes the company should follow, a major factor in reengineering is recognizing people as the critical element of the new knowledge-based organization. Responsibility within the organization is shifting from a "department" mentality to a "team" mentality. Managers "coach" rather than "supervise," and promotions and rewards are now more than ever based on results. While widespread reengineering still has a long way to go, the underlying concept behind it clearly encourages all employees to be self-directed.

An important effect of reengineering is that organizations tend to flatten out—that is, responsibility and decision making become more broadly dispersed throughout the organization. Since the portable executive thrives on responsibility, the flattened structure is ideal for the individual with a portable-executive mind-set. In addition, reengineering grants you the necessary freedom to feel comfortable functioning within a large organization, since what you are responsible for is within your control and you can actually see the outcome of your efforts. While the process of flattening organizational structures is wrenching, it is gratifying to see that many organizations are working hard to help their employees, their managers, and their executives make the transition to becoming more self-directed.

The Changing Role of Human Resources

Another significant shift that further supports the growth of portability is the change concerning human resources departments in the development of the new organization structure. In the past, human resources was often seen as a staff function that kept track of benefits, employment laws, and recruiting, while the "real" decisions were handled by the line management. As organizations have come to better appreciate that their employees are their primary assets, human resources departments are being considered part of the key decision-making teams. We are seeing human resources groups take leading roles in the structuring of self-directed work teams and introducing major efforts to assist employees in developing more independent approaches to their work.

Traveling the Electronic Highway

Communications expansion is contributing substantially to the acceptance of portability within organizations. Communications "highways," as they are now called, allow the dissemination of knowledge to the most remote parts of the organization in a way that empowers everyone. Since knowledge is the true asset, today's advances in communications technology give many more people within organizations the ability to use those assets in a productive manner. Having the appropriate information for your job is one thing; having information about how what you are doing affects the overall department, division, subsidiary, or company is considerably more powerful. This information frees you to apply your skills in ways that help you make significant contributions to an organization. Many companies work very hard to encourage employees at all levels to take advantage of the plethora of information made available to them to help them make decisions on their own, thus blurring the line between bosses and workers. This, once again, gives the individual a new sense of independence within the organization.

Everything Can Be Outsourced

Increases in outsourcing also support portability. The use of contract managers, accountants, lawyers, engineers, and consultants is steadily growing. Whole departments are now being out-sourced, such as purchasing, mail-room, and maintenance opera-tions, on the theory that consolidating special functions available to many clients would result in a greater efficiency. This trend, built on a company's desire for flexibility, will gain popularity and create increasing opportunities for portable executives on their own or as part of a company that offers out-services.

The Definition of Portability Is Still Evolving

While we can envision the system gradually (but definitely) accommodating flexible work relationships and the portable ex-ecutive mind-set, there are still a number of major obstacles to overcome before we can truly reap the full benefits of portability. To some extent, the issues themselves cannot be defined fully, because portability as a concept is still evolving and it's not clear how far it will go. What *is* clear is that an ever-increasing percent-age of the workforce at all levels will be moving from job to job or assignment to assignment much more frequently than ever be-fore. For some, this will mean working consistently as a contract or interim manager. For others, there will be longer "jobs," which may span years, but only a very few will be employed by one company for life. We will find more and more outsourcing com-panies emerging to spread the cost of these services over a num-ber of clients, thus allowing individuals to work for multiple companies while being employed by just one.

There are still some issues of significance with respect to portability that remain unaddressed. One very important issue confronting portable executives is the question of how they can obtain the benefits that were traditionally picked up by employ-ers. Employer group-benefit plans spread the cost over a large pool of people and thus hold costs down to a reasonable level. Currently, the United States is initiating a major debate on the whole area of health care with the goal of universal coverage through the private sector. It is not yet clear how the proposed new health care system will affect portable executives, but it is essential for the portable workforce to make its presence—and its health care needs—known.

Closely related to this is the issue of providing for old age. While the lifetime employment system was built on the assumption that most people would work for an organization for many years—if not for a lifetime—the problem of providing for old age becomes somewhat more complex in our shift toward portability. The portable executive, as a personal service business entity, needs to provide for his or her own retirement, but is not yet on the same footing as those who are employed by an organization. The portability of pension and retirement plans will prove to be a key issue for the contingent workforce as it continues to grow. Today, portable pension plans are available in many European countries and in Canada, but they are not yet fully available here in the United States. Portable pensions would allow the contingent workforce to build pension funds equivalent to those of corporate employees. Like the Clinton health care plan currently under debate, however, the development of portable pension plans will necessitate significant public debate and legislative effort.

Finally, we all must address the problem of chronic underutilization of the middle-management sector. Given the growth of technology, which has made large numbers of middle managers unnecessary, the fact is, there may not be enough work to go around. While this problem is certainly affected by the strength of our economy, as economic cycles are driven more by technology and less by individual labor, we will no doubt continue to be faced with the issue of chronic underutilization. It may be that the average number of hours worked over a lifetime will decline from 50,000 to 37,000 hours as more managers join the contingent workforce at earlier ages. And it is possible that increased competition and innovation within the portable community will result in the development of new services and products to spur the increase in the number of assignments. While there is no easy answer to the question of underutilization, it is clear that those who maintain their core skills at the highest level and market their capabilities aggressively will have a more consistent flow of assignments.

Another question that arises as the number of management jobs shrinks is how younger people will gain enough experience to be prepared for portability. Today's M.B.A.s are struggling to find entry-level jobs, and many of them are taking any job at any salary in order to gain experience. With such fierce competition, people are working hard to maintain and enhance their skills. However, it can also be argued that the younger generation will be far better prepared for portability, since they entered the workforce just as portability was beginning to transform it, and they already have to market themselves, develop their skills, and deal with the issues of financing when paychecks are not consistently forthcoming.

As the success of an organization becomes more dependent on the contingent workforce, one of the first issues that will need to be addressed is the distinction between "permanent employees" and "contract employees." We need to go beyond the obvious distinctions—such as benefits and retirement—to the status of the individual within the organization. How much confidential information, for instance, should an organization share with a consultant? What is the appropriate level of support to give a contract project manager? And, how much authority should an interim manager have?

While the road may not be smoothly paved for the portable workforce, it has the unique opportunity to create its own rules, its own identity, its own future. The door is open, the time is right, and the support is out there, readily available. All that remains is for you to search out what you like to do, create your business vehicle, and market and sell your skills aggressively to achieve a reasonable economic return and lifetime satisfaction. As Bud Titsworth put it:

I can't see myself ever working in a big organization again—this is too much fun. I go to my office early every morning to get geared up for the day, and almost every morning I find myself saying out loud, *"God, I love this!"*

NOTES

Unattributed quotations are from interviews conducted by the authors.

INTRODUCTION

p. 13. A feature article in *Fortune*: Louis S. Richman, "When Will the Layoffs End?" *Fortune*, September 20, 1993, p. 54.

p. 14. One woman in the press gallery: Gail Collins, "Career Survival, Star Trek Style," *Working Woman*, July 1993, p. 80.

CHAPTER ONE: A NEW PIECE OF AMERICANA

p. 24. On the Holmes "Schedule of Recent Experience": Martha Davis, Ph.D., Elizabeth Robbins Eschelman, M.S.W., and Matthew McKay, Ph.D., *The Relaxation & Stress Reduction Workbook* (Oakland, Calif.: New Harbinger Publications, 1982), p. 6.

p. 28. In 1991, 12.1 million: Robert E. Calem, "Working at Home, for Better or Worse," *New York Times*, April 18, 1993, sec. 3, p. 1.

CHAPTER TWO: THE NEW REALITY

p. 44. As William Davidson, a professor: Steve Lohr, "More Workers in the U.S. Are Becoming Hired Guns," *New York Times*, August, 14, 1992, p. 1.

p. 45. In a recent article quoting employees: Jill Andresky Fraser, "Life After I.B.M. Yes, and Often Sweet," *New York Times*, April 18, 1993, sec. 3, p. 25.

p. 45. When I left, I didn't: Ibid.

CHAPTER FOUR: BREAKING THE HABIT

p. 65. In an article entitled "Survivor": Judy Dash, "Survivor" *Family Circle*, March 16, 1993, p. 53.

NOTES

CHAPTER SIX: INVENTING YOUR BUSINESS

p. 101. To create what you must: Robert Fritz, *Creating* (New York: Fawcett, 1991), p. 163.

p. 113. "My sunk costs were more than": Ken Veit, "The Reluctant Entrepreneur," *Harvard Business Review*, November–December 1992, p. 40.

CHAPTER TEN: MARKETING AND SALES

p. 169. "According to the newsletter": *Clips & Tips*, July–August 1993, p. 1.

CHAPTER FOURTEEN: PORTABLE, AND LOVING IT

p. 226. "We are called to the place": Frederick Buechner to Trinity Institutes National Conference, "God with Us," January 23–24, 1990.

ACKNOWLEDGMENTS

In the course of our research we had the privilege of interviewing nearly a hundred executives who in one way or another were already on the road to becoming "portable." Time and again, executives opened their offices and their homes to us, spending long hours answering our questions and sharing the substantial wisdom they had gained on their own journeys as portable executives. We are deeply indebted to the men and women who gave so generously of their time and knowledge. They are the true pioneers of the portable workforce, and without them there would be no book.

We would also like to acknowledge the patience and cooperation of the principals of IMCOR who rearranged schedules in innumerable ways to free John up to interview and write. John would particularly like to thank Penny Holt, IMCOR's Director of Marketing, for help in convincing him that he really should share his ideas on "portability" with others. Two people in John's office made the daily drudgery of getting transcripts typed, phone calls answered, and faxes sent light work for both of us. There aren't enough words to thank Toni DeCarlo and Starlene Ralbovsky for their efforts, but they are the reason people write Acknowledgments in the first place.

Behind every book that is published are the experts in book publishing who shepherd the project through the long process from developing the initial proposal to the day the book appears in the bookstores. We are particularly indebted to our agent at Harold Ober & Associates, Henry Dunow, for his belief in the book and for his ever-available topnotch professional support.

Fred Hills and Laureen Connelly Rowland, our editors at Simon

& Schuster, have given their meticulous attention to our book at every stage. It was vastly improved by their comments, criticism, and support.

There are those people in our personal lives we wish to thank for their encouragement and support. Catharine will be forever indebted to Barbara Mulrine, Linda Peterson, Pamela Hart Rago, Jeanne DeMange, Mary Lea and Bill Blake, Jeanne Mettler and Elaine Balogh, who cheered her on and maintained her sense of humor. She would especially like to thank her brother, Christopher D. Henningsen, who found John Thompson and IMCOR for her while she was at work on the revision of Doubleday's *101 Best Businesses to Start*. And finally, Catharine would like to express her profound gratitude to Margaret T. Hayes, whose every thought and act has defined what it is to be a friend.

Catharine and John would also like to thank Bunny, Heather, and Bruce Thompson for graciously allowing Catharine to invade their home and family life for almost every weekend during the spring and summer of 1993. John particularly wants to thank his wife, Bunny, for her support during his personal transition to self-direction, as well as for her patience and tolerance throughout the eighteen-month process of writing this book.

INDEX

ABOUT
THE AUTHORS

JOHN A. THOMPSON is a visionary who saw in the 1980s that the relationship between companies and their employees was changing dramatically. He cofounded IMCOR, an interim management firm, to supply companies with the contract executives he knew they would increasingly need as they strived to stay lean and competitive. As the industry pioneer and spokesperson, Mr. Thompson has been a frequent speaker and is quoted extensively in the national media.

Mr. Thompson personally made the transition to a self-directed career when he took early retirement from KPMG Peat Marwick to start IMCOR. Previously, Mr. Thompson, as Chairman and Chief Executive Officer of KMG Main Hurdman, played a leading role in the merger of that firm with Peat Marwick Mitchell & Company, creating the world's largest public accounting firm.

Mr. Thompson currently serves as Chairman of IMCOR. He lives in Westport, Connecticut, with his wife, Bunny. They have two children, Bruce and Heather.

CATHARINE A. HENNINGSEN is an author, journalist, and business consultant whose work has appeared in major magazines and periodicals including the *New York Times*, *New Business Opportunities*, *Glamour*, and *American Bookseller*. Nominated for the Editor's Choice award in nonfiction in both 1982 and 1983, Ms. Henningsen holds an M.F.A. in writing from Goddard College and teaches in both the Master of Arts in Writing and the Master of Science in Organizational Management and Human Resource Development degree programs at Manhattanville College in Purchase, New York. She lives in Branford, Connecticut.